Don't Settle
for Less

MAIN STREET BOOKS

Doubleday

New York
London
Toronto
Sydney
Auckland

Don't Settle for Less

A Woman's Guide
to Getting a Fair
Divorce and Custody
Settlement

Beverly Pekala

A MAIN STREET BOOK
PUBLISHED BY DOUBLEDAY
a division of Bantam Doubleday Dell Publishing Group, Inc.
1540 Broadway, New York, New York 10036

MAIN STREET BOOKS, DOUBLEDAY, and the portrayal of a building with a
tree are trademarks of Doubleday, a division of Bantam Doubleday
Dell Publishing Group, Inc.

Don't Settle for Less was previously published in hardcover by
Doubleday, a division of Bantam Doubleday Dell
Publishing Group, Inc., in 1994. The Main Street Books edition
is published by arrangement with Doubleday.

The Library of Congress has cataloged the Doubleday edition as follows:
Pekala, Beverly.
    Don't settle for less : a woman's guide to getting a fair
divorce & custody settlement / Beverly Pekala — 1st ed.
        p.   cm.
    1. Divorce settlements—United States—Popular works.
2. Divorce—Law and legislation—United States—Popular
works.   3. Women's rights—United States—Popular works.
4. Child custody—Law and legislation—United States—Popular works.
KF535.Z9P45   1994   93-4795
346.7301'66—dc20   CIP
[347.306166]

ISBN 0-385-48211-6

Printed in the United States of America

First Main Street Books Edition: February 1996

10   9   8   7   6   5   4   3   2   1

To my parents:
for your constant love and support—
and for giving me an education,
for which I am endlessly grateful;
and

To my wonderful Robert,
for whom I am thankful
every single day

Contents

Contents

Introduction

This book grew out of a complaint that I've heard from women for years. After meeting with a divorce lawyer for the first time, they are often more confused then when they came in the door. For a person embarking on the road toward divorce, a lesson quickly learned is that the divorce system isn't nearly as simple as *L.A. Law* would have us believe, especially for women. I came to realize that women need a guide; something that gives them an advantage in a system that isn't always fair; a guide that can explain how to get that advantage in language that they can understand.

Throughout the book, I'll be referring to "the system" or "the divorce system" being unfair or discriminatory toward women and women with children. I'd like to clarify up-front exactly what I mean when I refer to "the system" being unfair. Am I referring to the judges or the laws themselves or to something else entirely? Most people realize that women and children get the short end of the stick after divorcing, yet it's often hard to put your finger on the cause.

The problem doesn't lie in the laws themselves. Although some laws result in discrimination, the fact is that discrimination exists in de facto rather than de jure form. The legal system contributes to this discrimination, not because the laws are inherently prejudiced, but because the legal system refuses to acknowledge that women and their children are playing the divorce game on an uneven field. The social and economic inequality in society is reflected in the courtroom and in settlements, where men receive more than women most of the time.

The legal system, composed of judges and juries, laws and lawyers, is fair, for the most part. In general, it bends over backward to guarantee that everyone is treated equally in the eyes of the law. Most laws are written to ensure that there is no bias against women.

Unfortunately, this system is fair only within the rarefied atmosphere of the courtroom. While a decision rendered in the hallowed halls may be just to both men and women, once they leave the courtroom and step onto the street, the decision immediately becomes unjust. The connection between an unequal society and an unfair divorce settlement is illustrated by the following:

A fifty-fifty split of marital property generally favors men. In most instances, men earn significantly more than women. Many times, men have established strong professional careers while women have been out of the work force taking care of the kids. Postdivorce, women generally have less income and/or potential for income than men.

The parent who receives custody loses out financially.

In most cases, women want and receive custody. Unfortunately, they often don't receive the child-support payments to which they're entitled. It's remarkably easy for men not to pay support. Self-employed men can hide a significant percentage of their income; men who remarry can "shelter" money in their new wives' names. Though it's true the courts can garnishee the wages of "deadbeat dads," they're often reluctant to furnish too much; judges know that many men would rather quit jobs than see a significant percentage go for support. Finally, there are men who don't make support payments because they can't. The economy has put many men out of work or forced them to take a lower-paying job; others have remarried and are trying to support two families.

Because of certain societal trends, men have an unfair advantage in custody battles. Consider this scenario: Mark and Julie engaged in a custody battle over three-year-old Joey. Mark's lawyer makes a compelling best-interest-of-the-child argument to the court, saying that after the divorce Mark intends to marry Cindy, who will stay home and take care of Joey. The lawyer demonstrates that Jill will have to work, and as a single parent, would have to farm Joey out to a childcare facility. Unstated in this argument is that Julie has stayed home with Joey for the past three years while Mark worked, placing Julie at a severe financial disadvantage.

Perhaps the most telling trend in this area is society's and the court's recognition that men are just as capable of raising children on their own as women. Courts do award custody to men instead of women, something that was unheard of not so long ago. The problem here is that men know this and use it as a bargaining chip. Although most men don't really want custody, they'll say they do and use it to negotiate a more favorable property settlement or child-support payment.

Men get better deals by default. For most divorcing couples, the man has more money than the woman. He can threaten her with a long, costly divorce battle; a battle she lacks the money to fight. As a result, she is likely to compromise her demands and settle out of court, even though she may have a very strong case.

Because of these inequities, the odds are that you'll receive a lot less than you're entitled to, unless you become aware of your rights and the way the system works.

Before I give you a sense of what you can do to remedy a basically unfair situation, I wish to clarify my point of view about five specific subjects:

First, I will be using the pronoun "she" when I refer to lawyers, as in "Your lawyer will rely on your input when she . . ." I use the feminine pronoun for two reasons: (1) I'm a woman lawyer, so it seems a natural reference. (2) "He/she" sounds awkward and the "he" is still first in the "he/she"; "she/he" sounds like a well-known author. Just because I'm using this feminine pronoun, however, doesn't mean that women shouldn't hire male lawyers. I know plenty of male attorneys who do excellent jobs of representing women. Nonetheless, I've found that women often feel more comfortable having a woman represent them.

Second, I don't believe that men are to blame for every divorce and that women are always innocent victims. I know there are cases in which women manipulate and take advantage of their husbands via the divorce process, in which they demonstrate an avarice and a disregard for the children's welfare that would do the worst sort of male chauvinist pig proud. I also recognize that my examples tend to portray women as the good gals and men as the bad guys. I do this only to illustrate situations which women should be aware of.

Third, some of my examples portray women as naïve and passive. I don't believe that all or most women are that way. The examples illustrate that naïveté and passivity are especially injurious during the divorce process and only by providing these examples can women see the types of behavior to avoid. I've also found that otherwise savvy women may take on these traits when relationships become rocky. In some ways, being naïve and being passive serve as denial mechanisms against the harsh reality of divorce.

Fourth, since the laws of each state differ, and are amended from time to time, it is imperative that you consult with a lawyer before filing for divorce. Do not blindly follow the well-intentioned advice you've received from friends, family or books such as this. Always seek the advice of an attorney *before* making any decision or taking any action.

Fifth, I hope that no reader of this book will use the advice I dispense for revenge. Vengeance may be a natural response in many cases, but it does not make for sound legal thinking or reasonable, rational results. It may cause you to ask for a bigger settlement than you can realistically expect or drag your family through a bitter trial that is as costly financially as it is emotionally.

Getting on with your life and living well is the best revenge.

Don't Settle for Less

SECTION · I

Chapter 1

Take This Woman: The Unfair Male Advantage

Just because you're a woman doesn't neces-
sarily mean that you'll get a rotten deal when you divorce.
There's certainly no law that says you will. In fact, divorce laws
generally place you on an equal footing with men. However,
the divorce system and social and economic trends handicap
women. The only way to give yourself a fighting chance is to
know more about the system than your spouse does, and use it
to your advantage.

If you're like most women going through a divorce, the
odds are that you'll receive a lot less than you're entitled to. If
you have children, they too will be cheated. Contrary to what
you may have thought or heard, the system does not treat men
and women as equals. If you doubt that statement, consider the
following statistics:

- Your chances of receiving alimony are less than 1
  in 5.[1]

3

- Less than one third of the women who were awarded alimony actually received the payments.[2]

- When men contest custody, they are successful 60 percent of the time.[3]

- It is unlikely that your husband will have to pay any part of your legal fees for the divorce.

- The number of single-mother households has jumped to almost 25 percent and is expected to increase.[4]

Even more frightening are the statistics showing how children fare after divorce:

- More than 22 million children never receive child support.[5]

- Over 9 million children have no health benefits.[6]

- Although granted visitation rights, millions of fathers spend no time with their children.[7]

- One out of every five American children lives in poverty.[8]

- Children of divorced parents are twice as likely to have significant behavioral problems as children of intact families.[9]

Do you think these statistics won't affect you? We all think divorce will never happen to us—until it does. The typical first marriage ending in divorce lasts just six years, according to the 1990 Report of the U.S. Census Bureau. Nationwide, your chances of being divorced are fifty-fifty, and more in some areas of the country. Even more shocking, first marriages last approximately two years longer than second marriages, according to the National Center for Health Statistics. If you are currently going through a divorce, you have found out firsthand how unfair the system is to women and children. The state of divorce in the 1990s is appalling.

The feminist movement has had an unexpected negative impact on how women fare in the divorce arena. Particularly since the 1960s, women have been raised to be independent and to rely only on themselves for financial security. Young women in their twenties and thirties are especially vulnerable to this line of thinking. However, the result is that a great many women do not obtain their fair share in a divorce settlement. They are much too quick to waive their rights, stating proudly that they can survive alone, without any help.

This is particularly true when it comes to the issue of alimony. Many women would walk on hot coals before asking for alimony, even when the facts show that it will be impossible for them to make ends meet without at least some short-term help. Some experts and others even argue that perhaps alimony should be eliminated completely. After all, women today are supposed to be self-sufficient and independent. Although men routinely decry the need for alimony, the domino effect of subsequent marriages has placed many second wives in the position of arguing against maintenance, since it is often the income of a second wife which is used to pay for the husband's alimony obligation to his first wife. A woman who did not receive alimony herself may end up with a husband who has this financial obligation to his former wife. The new wife is unhappy about taking on a debt that impacts on her own finances and, therefore, joins her husband in years of complaining about paying off the ex-wife.

Yet all these arguments lose sight of the real issue. That is, many women need financial assistance after a marriage dissolves so that they can get on their feet and become self-supporting. In many situations women wouldn't require alimony in the first place if it wasn't for the fact that they left their careers to become full-time mothers and homemakers. After sacrificing their careers for the good of the family, what do they end up with? A husband who doesn't understand why he should have to pay alimony, although his wife might have been out of the work force for ten, twenty, or even thirty years. He knows that she can't go back to her former career without additional training or education, and even then, getting a decent job may be difficult, or impossible, at her age.

Ask women in their forties, fifties, and even sixties how easy it is to get a job after having been married and at home for years. Considering their skills and the economy, most will tell you they're happy to get minimum-wage employment. Sadly, women at all levels of society end up with the same problem—many are too young for retirement and yet too old or poor to go back to school and get a good job. They're caught in the crunch.

Is it any surprise that husbands argue that the divorce court should split everything fifty-fifty and just let each party get on with their life? Of course, it's a lot easier for him to get on with his life. After all, he has probably worked at his job for ten or more years and earns a good income. Perhaps he's due to receive a raise or bonus, maybe another week or two of paid vacation, and is vested in the company profit-sharing plan.

6

What does his wife have to look forward to? Even if she's one of the lucky few to find a decent job, she's close to retirement but hasn't yet had the opportunity to build up her own pension plan or receive long-term medical benefits. When the divorce becomes final, she looks to the future with fear and trepidation.

Because of pay scales that favor men, women are generally at an economic disadvantage when a relationship ends—a fifty-fifty split of property is paradoxically unequal, since women have less earning power than men. In addition, the system fails to consider that many men still insist or encourage their wives to quit working, or stay at home full- or part-time. When the marriage ends, these women have been out of the work force for years and naturally have difficulty reentering it. In addition, the courts often fail to take into account the support women provide their spouses. How do you compensate a woman who has worked as a secretary for years to put her husband through medical school? When they divorce, he's pulling in a six-figure salary and she makes $30,000 annually.

It's no wonder the facts show that men survive divorce better than women. The case of Joan and Bill is typical. They had been married for fifteen years and had two girls, aged ten and seven. Joan didn't know how she would manage after the divorce became final. She hadn't worked in years and wasn't sure what type of employment she'd be able to find. Bill told her that after paying child support and the other bills he'd be squeaking by after the divorce was final. Much to her surprise, six months later Joan learned that Bill had purchased a new car and went to Cancún with his girlfriend. All the while, Joan had been working two jobs to make ends meet, since the child support was just not enough, even when Bill sent it to her on time. A year later Bill remarried and purchased a beautiful new home. Yet Joan was deeper in debt than the year before.

Sadly, Joan's case is typical. Numerous studies have shown that while a man's standard of living often improves after a divorce, a woman's standard of living, and that of her children, generally declines. Many factors account for these two very different results.

First, men are able to hide assets with relative ease during the divorce process (especially when women passively allow them to get away with it). They often have a nest egg they can tap after the divorce, and their support payments may reflect an artificially low income.

Second, divorced men without children have a better chance of entering a new relationship and reaping the financial benefits of living with someone (or remarrying) than divorced women with children.

Third, divorced men often have the time and freedom to make more money, while women have less freedom and time, because Dad is no longer around to share the household chores and child raising.

Fourth, and most important, men don't pay women child support that's sufficient to meet the needs of the children. It's not only that they don't pay enough; it's that often they don't pay at all. "Deadbeat dads" is the new term for these men who thumb their noses at their families and the legal system. Unfortunately, the system is structured so that it's possible for millions of men to get away with paying little or no child support, even after the court has ordered them to pay.

One reason for the current failure to receive support involves the employment loophole. Since a child-support order does not automatically follow a man from job to job, the easiest way for him to avoid paying support is simply to quit his job. By the time you find out where he's working, the law requires that you go back to court so another order can be entered which applies to his new job. Some men "coincidentally" lose their job after the order is entered and claim that they can't find work. Under the theory of "you can't get blood from a stone," the ex-husband figures that it will be too expensive and time-consuming for you to keep dragging him into court.

While some men blatantly refuse to pay support, most use a litany of excuses to explain why they won't send the support payment. Everything from "not being able to see the children" when they want to "having a few extra expenses" is used to explain why the check wasn't in the mail. However, the reality is that by failing to pay support these men are refusing to feed their own children and to keep a roof over their heads. As a result of nonpayment, many fathers have forced their children to become wards of the state and, in some cases, have made their children homeless. According to some studies, women and children are the fastest-growing segment of the homeless population in the United States.

The problem of deadbeat dads has reached such epidemic levels that most experts believe the federal government must get involved. National programs are currently being considered to ensure that children receive the payments they deserve. Possible new laws may include the establishment of a national child-support system and making the failure to pay a federal offense punishable by incarceration. If it seems that the child-support system is out of control, you're right.

What can be done to protect women and children in the

divorce process? The first step is knowing your rights—and the rights of your children. While your husband can probably afford to hire a good lawyer to represent him, chances are your finances won't allow for top-notch legal advice. It's no wonder: Women still earn 58 cents for every dollar earned by men. Even female lawyers earn only 63 cents for every dollar earned by male lawyers. This disparity in women's earning power immediately places women at a disadvantage.

Just as the unfairness of the system isn't confined to mothers, it's not limited by economic or social factors. White or black, rich or poor, suburbanite or city dweller, New Yorker or Nebraskan, women are still at a disadvantage when relationships end. Women everywhere have faced the same problem. During the marriage, you lived very comfortably. However, after divorce your standard of living has been reduced dramatically.

So far, you've heard the bad news. The good news is that it doesn't have to be this way. Women who know and assert their rights can beat the system. Every woman, no matter what the circumstances of her divorce, has various ways to even the odds. By opening your eyes and learning the system and the law, you will be able to find a strategy that will result in an equitable settlement for you and your children. Don't automatically assume that the divorce process will treat you fairly. It doesn't, and I'm continually amazed that more women aren't aware of the inequities. Those of us who represent wives in divorces can recount the horror stories of women who have been emotionally and financially abused by the divorce process. It's time to change women's approach to divorce, and this book is an attempt to help them do so. The advice and information contained in these pages has evolved out of hundreds of cases and years of experience. The recommendations in these pages are the same recommendations I've made to my clients. It has benefitted them and can benefit you.

In the following chapters, I'll provide you with many tools and techniques to protect yourself and your children before, during, and after the divorce. Some of the tactics focus on financial matters—property and money. Others involve issues relating to your children—custody, visitation, and paternity. You'll also find an appendix of useful "resources"—from women's legal organizations to helpful forms—specifically compiled for women going through divorces. Throughout the book, I offer suggestions to deal with the situations women find themselves in most frequently and answer the "What should I do?" questions that are most often asked. I hope to alert you to the traps and mistakes that frequently harm women before, during, and after divorces. They include:

The trap of assuming a pre- or postnuptial agreement is set in stone.

Falling for a spouse's threat that he wants the kids (and how to test if it's just a bluff).

Agreeing to your husband's suggestion for a no-fault divorce without analyzing with your attorney whether such a divorce is in your best interest.

Assuming your divorce settlement can never be changed and not understanding how to take advantage of postdecree court options.

There are many other mistakes and traps, as well as the ways to correct and avoid them, that will be discussed throughout the book. For now, however, start out with these basic tenets: Women should be proactive rather than reactive; they should try to take control of the divorce rather than let their spouses be in charge; they should fight for their rights rather than assume the court will make sure that a fair and equitable settlement is reached.

This theme is not based on the position that all men are jerks or that all women are saints. It's simply that I'm tired of seeing women and children get the short end of the stick. Women who know what they're up against and who educate themselves about how the system works consistently come out on top. I will share with you the knowledge necessary to help you and your children get what's fair—not what your husband thinks is fair.

References

1. Jane Bryant Quinn, *Newsweek,* 1/25/93.

2. U.S. Census Bureau, Report on Insurance and Divorce (1990).

3. Jane Bryant Quinn, *Newsweek,* 1/25/93.

4. Report of U.S. Commission on Interstate Child Support (1991).

5. Report of U.S. Commission on Interstate Child Support (1991).

6. Report of Employee Benefit Research Institute (a Washington research organization) (1991).

7. Federal Office of Child Support Enforcement, 14th Annual Report to Congress (1989).

8. U.S. Census Bureau, Children's Defense Fund (1991).

9. James Bray (psychologist at Baylor College of Medicine), *USA Today*, 12/9/92.

Chapter 2

Are You the Last One to Know You're Getting a Divorce?

You may be surprised to learn that the overwhelming number of divorce cases are filed by women. This doesn't mean, though, that more women want divorces than men. It has been my experience that women are often "forced" into filing for divorce.

I have heard the same story many times. A wife will come to my office in tears, saying she doesn't understand what is going on. She says that her husband told her out of the clear blue sky that he wants a divorce. However, she is perplexed because months have gone by and yet he hasn't done anything to get the divorce. In fact, he recently told her to find a lawyer and get the divorce rolling, even though he knows she doesn't want a divorce.

This situation is very common. Men will say they want a divorce and then expect their wives to take care of all the "legal details," including hiring a lawyer and filing the papers. Sometimes men say they are doing this out of respect for their wives, so the wife can say that she filed against him rather than vice versa. Before she knows it, she's sitting in a lawyer's office not knowing what has hit her.

She's there, but she never saw it coming. She didn't notice any of the classic warning signs. She was wearing the "perfect marriage" blinders.

The Ozzie and Harriet Marriage

Carol thought she had the perfect marriage. Bob was a hard-working husband who always gave her enough money to run the household. He worked long hours but spent as much time with the children as he could. Carol was shocked when Bob sat her down, told her he wanted a divorce, and presented her with an agreement dividing up everything they owned.

After Carol saw a lawyer, she began telling her friends about the divorce. Much to her surprise, everyone else had suspected that something was wrong—everyone except Carol.

Carol missed many of the classic warning signs that are a prelude to divorce. She didn't notice what everyone else did. I know what you're thinking—it won't happen to you. You think Carol was just stupid, but you would definitely know if something was going on. Well, everyone thinks that it can't happen to them. Believe me, I've had some extremely intelligent women in my office crying their eyes out. They were stunned when their husband "suddenly" asked for a divorce.

Most people do notice some changes. Carol realized that money seemed to be a little tighter than usual and that Bob was spending less time at home. In fact, Carol asked Bob about these things, and he gave her a perfectly reasonable explanation. Why did Carol buy that explanation? It wasn't because Carol was particularly gullible or naïve. In fact, in all other aspects of her life, Carol demonstrated a healthy skepticism and sophistication. But when it came to the possibility of divorce, Carol's natural screening mechanism deserted her. Her desire to preserve the marriage, a natural and admirable desire in other circumstances, allowed her to fall for Bob's cover story. While some women would spot Bob's lies in less time than it would take for him to call his girlfriend from the phone in his study, most would not. I've found that many women are like Carol, and to a certain extent such attitudes are inevitable. Women with children especially are acutely aware of the negative effects of divorce on kids, and want to deny there's a problem for their children's sakes, if not for themselves.

Ultimately, however, denial serves neither the woman nor the kids. Ignoring the warning signs of divorce can have devastating consequences, not only emotionally but legally.

The Warning Signs

In most cases, warning signs appear before a divorce. These signs lead a reasonable person to ask whether their marriage is in trouble. While the warning signs don't necessarily mean that your spouse wants a divorce, they are usually a signal that your spouse is either planning for divorce or thinking of separating from you. The signs may also mean that your spouse is having an affair or has a substance-abuse problem. The most common warning signs are:

Money disappearing, assets being sold

Although your expenses haven't gone up, it seems there is less money available than there used to be. You can't quite figure out where the money is going. At first, it isn't much, maybe $50 or $100 every month or so. After six months, you think more money is missing.

Then your husband tells you (or you find out on your own) that he has closed a savings account or cashed in some bonds. He says there were more bills than you realized. This comes as a surprise, but he assures you that the situation is temporary and not a big deal.

"Skimming" money is nothing new. Spouses have been doing it for years. If your husband is planning on leaving, he wants to save enough money to rent an apartment, buy some furniture, and hire a lawyer. It is not unusual for a spouse to take a year or two before he has "skimmed" enough money so he can finally move out and get a divorce. Chapter 6 will explore in detail how your lawyer can find out where the money went. Through the use of depositions, subpoenas, and other discovery tools, you'll find out how much of your marital assets were used by him for his own, nonmarital purposes.

Change of lifestyle

Your husband always came home from work at about the same time. Now, it's hard to say when he'll be home. Perhaps he is traveling more than he used to. After a while, he doesn't come home on the weekend from out of town, since he'll just have to fly back on Monday.

Maybe he used to talk a lot about work. Now, he never talks about work (or vice versa). If your husband suddenly has a new wardrobe and new friends, ask yourself what could be causing this change in behavior. Although the explanation may be perfectly innocent, you owe it to yourself to explore the reasons behind any dramatic change in his life. If he has started exercising or lost weight, it could be a sign that he simply wants to get in shape, or that he's preparing to go out into the world on his own, as a single man.

Change of behavior with children

Your husband used to be a workaholic. He'd leave early in the morning and return late at night. He was always too tired to spend time with the children, and when he was with the children, he seemed cranky and irritable.

Now, he has become father of the year. Not only does he spend time with the children at home, he takes them out to sporting events and to the movies. All of a sudden, the children can't wait for Dad to get home.

No doubt you are happy with your husband's new attitude. You don't even question why he's suddenly spending so much time with the kids, and if you do, you chalk it up to his guilt at having ignored them for so long. Well, think again. His sudden change of behavior is all part of a carefully designed plan, one which will put him in a better light in the eyes of the divorce court. Chapter 7 will discuss, in depth, custody and visitation issues and how you can protect yourself from getting stuck with an agreement designed to favor your husband.

Do you see your life in any of these warning signs? If any of the questions sound familiar, ask whether your spouse could be considering divorce. Don't automatically say, "Not my husband." Look at the *facts*.

Of course, each of the items listed above could be explained in many ways. Just because your husband has a new wardrobe doesn't necessarily mean he's seeing another woman. On the other hand, have you noticed any other warning signs? How many signs apply to your life? Two or three? Maybe more?

If so, give serious thought to your relationship. Even if all the warning signs are there, don't assume that divorce is inevitable. Consider all of your options:

1. Talk to your husband about seeing a priest, minister, or marriage counselor. It's very possible that your husband hasn't explored whether the marriage can be saved. My experience has been that approximately half of divorcing couples have been through some type of marriage counseling. Even if counseling doesn't save a marriage, it often provides an opportunity for each party to vent their frustrations and to get through the emotional suffering. As a result, the divorce itself is often quicker and easier, since they're focusing on legal issues and not emotional ones.

2. Consider asking your husband if he wants a divorce or has thought about it. Many clients are amazed that all they

have to do is ask the question. The husband is relieved his wife figured it out. Now he doesn't have to worry about how to begin the conversation he's been dreading and tell her the truth.

Don't ask this question, though, unless you are prepared for his answer, both emotionally and practically. If your husband admits that he's unhappy and wants an immediate divorce, you may be financially and legally devastated. Therefore, consider saying nothing to your husband until you see a lawyer. The section at the end of this chapter entitled "Consult with an attorney" will help you choose an appropriate time to confront your husband about whether he wants a divorce and develop a game plan to protect you and your children.

The Legal Consequences of Ignoring the Warning Signs

Ignoring the warning signs can be dangerous, emotionally and legally. The fact is, you have been set up. The problem with ignoring the warning signs is that you have allowed your husband to have a very valuable commodity on his side. That commodity is time. While you are unaware of your husband's true intentions, he has had the time to set you up financially or otherwise. For example, he had the ability to sell your assets, manipulate your money, and wipe you out financially. He has also had the time to change his image, show that he is now a perfect father, and take custody of the children away from you.

Here's how it works. By the time your husband admits that he wants a divorce, he has disposed of all of your assets, leaving you with nothing. He probably paid off his charge-card balances, so he has no debt in his name. However, you still have bills in your name. When it comes time to divide up the debt, you may be stuck with debts in your name, and yet he's free and clear. Now you're left with large bills, and he has good credit.

If he sold any assets, it may be impossible to get your share of the value of those assets during the divorce. To a certain extent, it's like closing the barn door after the horse is out. Tracing where all the money went after selling the assets is a difficult, time-consuming task. Consider how hard it would be for you to account for every dollar you've spent in the last year. The fact is, it may cost you more in legal fees to be reimbursed for what was taken than what you'd end up with, and that's even if you can prove what he did.

Of course, learning that you may be wiped out financially is enough of a shock. Worse than that is learning you've been set up to lose custody of your children. Has your husband started spending more time with the children? Has he become involved in Boy Scouts or their athletic events (although you used to have to beg him to go)? Fathers being counseled by men's rights attorneys are told to spend a great deal of time with the children. The strategy is simple: Threaten to take sole custody of the children and make it look like you're serious. Most mothers would do anything to keep custody of their children—even if it means giving away every dollar they're entitled to. This is exactly what the husband and his lawyer are hoping for. During the negotiation, they drop their request for custody and you are left with very little financially. It's an old story. Unfortunately, women fall for this far too often.

And that's if you're lucky. Some men are so adamant about not paying child support that they truly wage an all-out war for custody of the children. If they're serious, they may spend years in planning. Some men are so vindictive they want to wipe out their spouse completely. They want the money and the children. Most importantly, they want to feel they "won."

What to Do Before You Call the Lawyer

What happens if you spot some of the warning signs? You don't automatically want to assume the worst, and yet you aren't sure what to do. Here are some suggestions.

1. Talk to your husband

Before jumping to conclusions, talk to your husband. Ask him the questions that have been keeping you awake at night. What looked like a warning sign might prove to be absolutely nothing. On the other hand, your husband might give you answers that are vague or just don't make sense. Hear him out and really listen to what he says. The answers might surprise you.

2. Become your own private detective

You've asked the questions and don't like the answers you've been given. What now? It's time to investigate. A wife who has taken off the "blinders" and is ready to accept reality can be a good detective. If money seems to be missing, find out exactly where it has gone. Don't settle for comments like "Honey, you just wouldn't understand." Don't take no for an answer. Call the banks and the credit-card companies. Make it your mission to verify the facts. Remember, you're entitled to this information. You have a right to know.

3. Hire a private investigator

If you've done all you can, but still can't find out what's going on, it might be time to hire a professional. Women usually hire private detectives to find out whether their husband is cheating on them. The investigator will place your husband under surveillance for a week or more. At the end of that time, the investigator will give you a report showing where your husband has been and whom he has been with. If you wish, the investigator will take photographs. Hiring a private detective is an expensive proposition. Before doing so, think carefully about whether you want to have your husband followed and whether you are ready to see and hear the results of the investigation.

4. Consult with an attorney

If you asked questions and investigated, but don't like what you've learned, it's time to make an appointment with a lawyer.

This doesn't necessarily mean you'll be filing for divorce immediately or that you'll have to run home and tell your husband the marriage is over. The purpose in visiting a lawyer at this juncture is to obtain an objective opinion about your husband's conduct. If your lawyer concurs that the facts show that your husband is likely to leave, she'll counsel you to first establish a game plan that will favor you and your children in the event a divorce does occur. This plan will include a variety of actions that you should take. For example, she'll probably tell you to begin paying off debts in your name and applying for your own credit cards. You should also put money aside for attorney's fees and spend more time with the children. Don't feel guilty about doing whatever is necessary to protect yourself. Remember, you have been forced into a corner by your husband and may be left with nothing unless you fight fire with fire.

Don't wait until you've seen every warning sign on the list before you see a lawyer or develop a game plan. By that time, the damage could have been done. Waiting could jeopardize your future and the future of your children. Don't let yourself and your children become victims.

Chapter 3

Women and Lawyers: Choosing a Legal Relationship That Will Give You an Edge

Introduction

For many women facing the possibility of divorce, the most frightening thing to do is see a lawyer or even call a lawyer. To do that would make the divorce too real.

Do any of these excuses sound familiar?

"Why should I spend money on a lawyer? My husband and I are just going through a rough period. We'll be able to work out our problems."

"I already know what my rights are. I talked to my friend Joan, who went through a divorce a couple of years ago. She told me what I should do."

"I don't have to get my own lawyer. My husband said that he and I could both use the lawyer who did our real estate closing. After all, we don't have that much and we've basically agreed on almost everything."

In my experience, most women find it very difficult to even call an attorney. Perhaps it is the commitment women bring to marriage. Women take marriage very seriously and won't give up easily. To most people, seeing a lawyer means giving up. It is far easier to talk to friends, acquaintances at work, sisters-in-law, anyone except a lawyer. Women find it very difficult to admit their marriage is in trouble. They tend to ignore the warning signs. Society teaches women to be "rescuers." We have been brought up to believe that we can fix the problems in the relationship. Look prettier, cook a better dinner, and everything will work out. The needs of our family come first, and we consider our own needs last, if at all. For women, seeing a lawyer means facing the fact that we can't fix what's wrong.

Most people who have been through a divorce will be delighted to spend hours telling you about what happened to them and giving you what I call "barroom" advice. Hearing about these experiences is fine. Just remember, when you're through listening to the stories, SEE A LAWYER. Only then will you find out the law as it applies to *your* case and what you should do in your particular circumstance.

The longer you put off seeing a lawyer, the greater the chance that your husband will have an edge. Oftentimes the spouse who is considering divorce will see a lawyer very early on; perhaps a year or more before they actually follow through.

Just as in any other area, the person who gets professional advice first has an edge. For your sake and the sake of your children, you want to make sure that you are the one who has an edge.

How to Find a Good Lawyer

Okay, you've made the decision to see a lawyer. But how do you find a good one? When looking for a lawyer, many sources can be of help:

Local bar association referral services

These organizations will recommend several attorneys in your area who specialize in divorce. Bar associations may also give you other information about the attorney, such as the number of years she has been in practice and the attorney's areas of specialization. Often, women are most comfortable having a female lawyer represent them. Therefore, I recommend contacting the Women's Bar Associations in your area. Consult Appendix A for a list of these organizations.

Recommendations from divorce support groups

Such groups often have a list of attorneys that members of the group have worked with and recommend. Additionally, divorce support groups often have attorneys speak at their meetings. Contact one or more of these groups. It may be possible for you to attend a meeting at which a panel of lawyers will be present. This will provide you with an opportunity to hear from several attorneys and perhaps briefly discuss your case with one of the lawyers, for no charge.

Friends and family

Like finding a doctor or other professional, word of mouth is often the best source for finding good representation. However, be cautious. No two cases are identical. Just because your friend's lawyer did a great job for her doesn't mean that the same lawyer is right for you. Talk to people whose cases involved issues similar to yours.

Law school legal clinics

If you cannot afford a private attorney, you may contact the legal assistance foundation in your area or the local law school. Law schools often have legal clinics, which have senior law students working with a supervising attorney. These legal clinics generally handle cases such as landlord-tenant disputes and simple divorces. There may be no fee or a small fee for their services, if you qualify. Obtain the names of the law schools in your area and call each of their legal clinics. A supervising attorney or student will talk with you about your case. Have available the approximate amount of your income per year and a brief summary of the issues involved in your case.

Contacting the Lawyer

Now that you have the names of several lawyers, you aren't quite sure what to do. You don't know whether to call them or make an appointment to see them, and you don't know what you'll say when you do talk to them.

Most attorneys will not discuss a new case with you over the phone. It will be necessary for you to make an appointment to discuss your situation face to face. I suggest that you call at least two lawyers and make appointments to see each of them. Obviously, you want an opportunity to hear what more than one person has to say. Your lawyer will play an important role in your life. Make sure that you will be comfortable disclosing confidential and personal information to your lawyer and her staff.

When you call the attorney's office, ask for her secretary or paralegal. Many lawyers have their office staff make appointments with new clients. Tell the assistant that you have been referred to this lawyer for a divorce and that you want to schedule an initial consultation with her. Find out whether the attorney has evening or weekend hours if that is important to you.

Sample questions that will help you select the attorney who is right for you are provided later in this chapter.

Attorney's Fees

True or false: In most divorce cases, the husband will be responsible for paying his wife's attorney's fees as well as his own?

If you answered true, you are laboring under one of the biggest myths about divorces. Many years ago, the law did require that a husband pay for part, or all, of his wife's attorney's fees. Those days are gone. Today, courts often hold each party responsible for payment of their own fees and costs.

One of the most difficult aspects for women in divorce cases is coming to grips with the issue of attorneys and their fees. Most women have never hired a lawyer before. As a result, they don't understand the most basic issues involved in hiring a lawyer and paying for the lawyer's services. For example, women often don't realize that lawyers charge for their time based upon an hourly fee. Women are often shocked to learn that every time they call their lawyer they are being charged. In general, people unfamiliar with hiring lawyers fail to realize that they are charged for all time that is spent working on a case, which includes telephone time, travel time, and time spent waiting in court before your case is called. The fact that the husband may not be responsible for payment of fees also comes as a great shock to most women. If the husband won't have to pay, they wonder where the money will come from. Often, women don't have cash available and don't have bank accounts or savings accounts in their own names.

Don't kid yourself. It is more difficult to find an attorney to take the side of the "poorer spouse" in the divorce. However, women cannot allow themselves to be paralyzed by the fear that no one will take their case and that they are "stuck." There are attorneys who will work with you and are willing to be flexible on the issue of payment of fees. Some attorneys will agree to take a lower retainer and to accept installment payments. Talk openly with your lawyer about the possible methods of financing your divorce. Female attorneys who mainly represent wives in divorces are often more flexible on this issue.

Obviously, the inability to pay fees is something of great concern to women. Every person wants to obtain the best legal representation available. Yet how can you compete if your finances are limited? First, become aware of how to hire a lawyer and how a lawyer charges for her services.

1. The initial consultation

What I am about to tell you is the most important piece of advice you will ever receive. Almost all attorneys provide an initial consultation at *no cost*. Women who are without funds have the same ability as others to obtain quality legal advice for no charge.

The no-cost consultation makes good business sense for the lawyer and provides an excellent opportunity for the client. You have the ability to discuss your case for free and learn how the attorney would proceed if you decide to hire her. It gives you the opportunity to determine whether you would feel comfortable working with this person. The consultation is helpful for the attorney as well. It allows the lawyer to hear the facts of your case and determine whether she is qualified to handle your case and will choose to represent you.

The consultation usually lasts an hour, so use your time wisely. Don't squander your time telling the lawyer what a jerk your husband has been all these years. Come to the meeting prepared with a summary of the most important facts about your case and have questions ready as well. (Sample questions are provided later in this chapter.) If you require additional time, the attorney will probably ask that you begin paying an hourly fee.

2. How do lawyers charge for their services?

Most lawyers charge between $100 and $200 per hour. You are responsible for the time your lawyer spends on your case. This includes time in court, on the telephone, and traveling to the courthouse. Some lawyers charge a flat fee for cases, regardless of the number of hours spent on your file. However, few lawyers charge by the case, since it is impossible to predict the number of hours your situation will require.

3. What is a retainer?

Attorneys commonly require a retainer before they will begin working on your case. A retainer is a sum of money that you prepay, usually from $500 to several thousand dollars. As the lawyer works on your case, she will charge her time against this retainer, based on the hourly fee. When there is nothing left of the retainer, you will begin paying your lawyer on a monthly basis for any work done on your case.

4. Don't be "penny wise and pound foolish"

Before starting the divorce process, you must accept that there will be legal fees and court costs associated with the divorce. Do not be "penny wise, and pound foolish" when it comes to hiring a lawyer. If necessary, borrow the money from family or friends. Take an advance on your charge cards or try to get a loan from a bank. Do whatever is necessary to obtain the funds to hire a good lawyer. Consider the money you are spending now to be an investment. Lawyers are often amazed that a client will balk at paying legal fees but think nothing of charging hundreds of dollars on their charge card for something much less important. Just as with anything else, you get what you pay for. Don't wait until after the divorce is final to see that in the long run skimping on attorney's fees cost you more than you realized. Consider the alternatives: Receiving less child support than you're entitled to, selling your house, or becoming responsible for your husband's debts. Retain a good lawyer. You can't afford not to.

The First Meeting

You've made the appointment and the day has finally arrived. You're going to see at least one lawyer today. The following list will help you prepare for that first meeting.

Bring a list of your assets, liabilities, income, and expenses. In order for your lawyer to give you an accurate assessment of your case, she must know your financial condition. List everything you and your husband own, either jointly or separately, including real estate, automobiles, bank accounts, and retirement funds. You should also provide a detailed list of all monthly expenses and all sources of income, including child support you may be receiving. (A sample income/expense statement is shown in Appendix B.)

If you can't have all of this information for your attorney at the first meeting, try to put together as much as possible. Sometimes women are not aware of all the assets or debts or of the amount of income or expenses. If your husband has handled the finances, you may not have this information. Don't feel stupid or embarrassed. Your lawyer will uncover this information once you have filed for divorce.

Ask your lawyer about any problems or questions that concern you. Remember what we were told in school—there is no such thing as a stupid question. Oftentimes the issue that bothers you the most will turn out to have no impact on the divorce at all. Don't hold back. Your lawyer can't read your mind and needs to know what is troubling you.

Communicate honestly with your lawyer. You must tell your lawyer about your marriage and why you are now discussing a divorce. Don't leave out information because you are embarrassed or don't think it is important. Your lawyer is not there to judge you or to pry into personal matters. However, in order to help, she must know all of the facts relating to your case. Err on the side of telling too much, not too little. Sooner or later, keeping your lawyer in the dark will hurt your case.

Discuss fees and costs. It is extremely important that you and your attorney reach an understanding regarding the attorney's fees and costs relating to your case. Today most lawyers have an agreement which they will review with you and ask you to sign. This agreement clearly explains the representation they will provide to you and the fees and costs for those services. If necessary, take the agreement home and read it. As with any other document, don't sign it unless you thoroughly understand your rights and responsibilities.

Discuss the game plan. Once you have retained the attorney, you should discuss short-term and long-term planning. Before you leave her office, make sure that you have a clear understanding of what is likely to happen in the next month or two. Usually your lawyer will give you "homework." For example, she may tell you to close certain accounts or to pay certain bills. Remember, you must do your part in order for the advice to be worthwhile.

One last note about the game plan. If the lawyer is telling you only good things, such as "everything is going to work out in your favor" or "We're going to get everything and your husband will get nothing," you should be extremely suspicious. It is very rare that one person gets everything and the other receives nothing. Use some common sense. Ask yourself if this seems realistic to you or if the attorney might be telling you this only to get your business. If any of these questions cross your mind, even for an instant, get a second opinion before going any further.

Specific questions to ask your lawyer

The following are common questions that you should ask an attorney before retaining one:

1. How long have you been in practice and how many divorce cases have you handled?

2. How often do you represent the wife as opposed to the husband?

3. How many cases have you handled involving the specific issue in my case (custody, tax matters, etc.)?

4. Will you be the only attorney handling my case? If not, who else will be working on my case and when will I meet them?

5. How long will it take to resolve my case? How often does it usually take?

6. How many cases are resolved by settlement negotiation and how many actually go to trial?

7. How will I be billed? By the hour or by the case? How often will I receive a bill? Will I be charged at different rates for in-court versus out-of-court time?

8. What are your normal business hours and when are you easiest to reach? If you are not available, to whom should I direct my questions?

The Relationship Between You and Your Lawyer

You have now retained an attorney. You feel comfortable working with this person and have started down the road toward becoming divorced. Anyone who has been down this road knows the process can be a slow and painful one. The relationship between you and your lawyer may last months or even years. You will be working closely with your lawyer and discussing very personal matters. Before beginning this journey, you and your lawyer should clearly understand your rights and responsibilities.

First, let me share some basic rules for being a good client.

Rule 1. EVERYTHING IS NOT AN EMERGENCY; OR, YOUR LAWYER IS NOT ON CALL TWENTY-FOUR HOURS A DAY, SEVEN DAYS A WEEK.

This is the first and most important rule of being a good client. Obviously, there are times when a true emergency might arise and you need to speak to your lawyer. Unless your lawyer has specifically given you a home telephone number, don't call your lawyer at home. Your lawyer has business hours, usually 9 A.M. to 5 P.M., Monday through Friday. In almost all cases, your lawyer cannot do anything until the courthouse opens at 9 A.M.

As a general rule, the matter that you consider an emergency is one that can wait—perhaps an hour, or perhaps until tomorrow. It is possible that the "emergency" can wait forever, because there is no emergency. Please understand that there are many situations that will upset you but don't call for legal action. Before you pick up the phone, ask yourself whether this is actually a legal emergency. Remember, don't be like the little boy who cried wolf.

Also, remember that each time you call your lawyer, you are being charged for time. Do not be surprised when you receive a large bill because you have called your lawyer three times a day for the past month. Write down all your questions so you can review them during one telephone conference or personal meeting.

Rule 2. YOUR LAWYER IS NOT A PSYCHOLOGIST.

Divorce is certainly an emotionally stressful time. Indeed, it may be the most stressful period of your life. Although therapy is not needed by everyone, many people benefit from seeing a counselor or therapist during the divorce process. Don't expect your lawyer to be a psychologist. Although your lawyer is sensitive to your situation, she is not trained to provide expertise regarding your emotional condition and you have not hired her for this purpose. However, because of the very close relationship between you and your lawyer, many women feel most comfortable hiring a female lawyer. They often feel that another woman will be more sensitive to the issues and personal concerns raised during the divorce process.

Rule 3. COMMUNICATE HONESTLY WITH YOUR LAWYER.

Open communication applies from the moment you first meet your lawyer right up until the day your divorce becomes final. There is a great deal of information that your lawyer can only know if you tell her. Women often have a difficult time completely confiding in their lawyer (particularly if the lawyer is a man). Women are more sensitive to their real or perceived transgressions and often believe that the slightest admission to their lawyer will touch off a series of events that will result in losing custody of their children. Women often fear that conduct long in the past will come back to haunt them, such as having used drugs in college. Unfortunately, we know that society expects a higher standard of behavior from women than men.

As a general rule, the "secret" you are keeping from your lawyer will not have any effect on your case—as long as you disclose it to your lawyer in the beginning. If you do not tell your lawyer the whole story, or if you actually lie to her, you are only cheating yourself. By the time your lawyer learns the whole truth, the damage may already have been done and it may be too late for her to help you. If you can't bring yourself to talk about something that is particularly difficult, send her a letter explaining the situation.

Rule 4. THIS IS NOT *L.A. LAW.*

You might be thinking, "Oh, come on, we all know TV isn't the real world." Well, you would be surprised by the number of people who truly believe that their case should be handled just like they saw on television. I have heard clients say, "Why did my lawyer do such and such? That's not how they did it on *L.A. Law.*"

The moral of the story is: Don't believe everything you watch. One of the things not to believe is that every attractive divorce lawyer propositions his clients. Though there are Arnie Beckers out there, they are, thankfully, a decided minority. Still, a few words of warning are in order. First, it is true that the potential for a relationship exists; combine one emotionally distraught woman and one kind and helpful lawyer who salves the woman's damaged ego and gives her guidance in a time of need, and sparks can ignite. Just as patients fall in love with their doctors, clients fall in love with their lawyers. I would strongly urge you not to let that happen. For one thing, it provides a lawyer with the wrong kind of motivation; he probably figures that you'll sleep with him as long as the divorce process lasts, so it's in his selfish interest to keep the process going as long as possible. Second, if you are becoming overly dependent on your lawyer because of a sexual relationship, you're probably going to end up with a double divorce. Not only will you go through the emotional trauma of separating from a husband, but after the divorce is over, there will be the trauma of separating from your lawyer.

I haven't found romantic relationships between lawyers and clients to be common. But if you see one developing, run from it as fast as you can.

Rule 5. YOUR LAWYER DID NOT CREATE THE SYSTEM AND CAN-
NOT CHANGE THE SYSTEM.

This is an extremely important point, especially for women.
In many ways, the legal system is particularly unfair to women,
since the system is slanted in favor of the spouse with the
greater financial resources, which is usually the husband. Your
lawyer knows all too well the various injustices against women
inherent in the system.

Don't blame your lawyer if the judge's calendar is booked
for the next month or if you show up in court only to find that
your case was transferred elsewhere. Your lawyer cannot
change the rules; she can only work within them.

You may wonder about the consequences of violating the
"good client" rules. Well, failure to follow these rules may result in your lawyer "firing" you. Just as you can discharge your
lawyer (more about that later), your attorney can choose to stop
representing you and withdraw from your case. This usually
happens if you fail to communicate with your lawyer or consistently fail to follow her advice. It may also occur if you cannot
or will not pay your bill. Following the good client rules will
avoid the problem of being fired by your lawyer.

Now that you know the rules for being a good client, you're
probably asking yourself what responsibilities your lawyer has.
Lawyers have many responsibilities, but they all fall under the
one "Golden Rule" for lawyers.

THE GOLDEN RULE: COMMUNICATE WITH YOUR CLIENT.

The most common complaint against lawyers is their failure to communicate with clients. Although lawyers are sometimes guilty of this charge, oftentimes it is for good reason. Your attorney might have been in court longer than expected, or might have had to go out of town suddenly. For some lawyers, emergencies are more the rule in their practice than the exception. When a client calls a lawyer with an emergency, the lawyer must stop working on other matters to attend to the problem. Frankly, some lawyers fail to communicate because their clients have violated Rule 1 for clients. (Remember that one?) When the lawyer receives the sixth "emergency" phone call from a particular client in two days, she may not respond very quickly.

However, this still does not relieve the lawyer of the responsibility to help the client and answer her questions. If it is not possible for your attorney to call you personally, someone from the office should contact you, advise when the lawyer is expected to be available, learn the nature of your problem or question, and communicate a response as soon as possible.

If you are not receiving frequent communications from your attorney, it might be time to change lawyers. How often your lawyer communicates with you depends upon the status of your case. As a general rule, you should be in contact with your attorney's office at least once a month, whether in writing or by phone. At particularly difficult stages of your litigation, such as when a major hearing or trial is scheduled, it might be necessary for your lawyer to speak with you every week, or even every day. However, this is the exception to the rule. Only in situations of extreme emergency should daily or weekly communication be required.

Firing Your Lawyer

There is one rule about your lawyer you should never forget. A client ALWAYS has the right to discharge her attorney. You do not need a reason. You can discharge your attorney at any time. Of course, you will be responsible for payment of any work done on your case before the time of the discharge.

Unfortunately, women are often unaware of this rule. As a result, many women have been represented by a lawyer who they believe wasn't acting in their best interests. If you think your lawyer is "giving away the store" to your husband, get a second opinion. If the attorney is recommending a custody or visitation arrangement that you have clearly stated you won't agree to, get a second opinion.

Naturally, you should discharge your attorney only after careful consideration and after receiving at least one other opinion. Don't be like the patient who goes from doctor to doctor until he finds someone to tell him what he wants to hear. As a client going through an emotionally painful situation, it may be difficult to distinguish the difference between bad advice and advice that you just don't want to hear. As a general rule, if you receive the same advice from two lawyers, or more, you can be assured that your lawyer's recommendation was good advice, albeit difficult to accept. Another signal that your lawyer is not off track is the recommendation that a judge may make at a pretrial or at the time of a hearing. If the judge's remarks or decision confirms what your lawyer has told you, it's time to stop shopping and accept the situation.

Remember, oftentimes the lawyer you consider the most difficult is the one who is the most honest with you.

Chapter 4

Domestic Violence

There are a myriad of reasons that people divorce, including adultery, alcoholism, and abandonment. However, no reason is more compelling than physical abuse. When I first began practicing divorce law, I was amazed to learn the number of women who were victims of domestic violence. Women who came to me to discuss a divorce rarely volunteered that they were victims of abuse. I usually found out accidentally, during the course of our initial interview. It didn't take me long to realize that the first question a lawyer must ask the client is whether she or her children have been abused. The answer determines the legal and practical steps that must be taken to protect you and your children prior to obtaining the divorce, and may change the outcome of the divorce itself.

If you have been a victim of domestic violence, you didn't "ask for it" and you certainly didn't deserve it. The fact is, your husband's behavior will not stop until he realizes he has a problem and gets professional counseling. Until that happens, you cannot allow yourself and your children to remain vulnerable to the abuse. You already know that abuse doesn't happen just once. The pattern repeats itself and the violence gets worse over time. Don't accept the "morning after" promises from your husband that he will never hurt you or the children again.

The good news is there are many people who are anxious to help you and your children. Before we talk about getting help, the first step is recognizing the problem. You may not even realize that you or your children have been victims of domestic violence.

What Is Domestic Violence?

Domestic violence includes many different types of abuse. Even if your husband has never laid a hand on you, he can still be guilty of domestic violence. Abuse involves not only physical violence but psychological abuse as well.

Physical abuse, slapping, kicking, beating, striking, biting, and any other such physical actions always constitute domestic violence. If your husband has been physically abusive to your children, but not to you, he may be guilty of domestic violence and child abuse.

Psychological abuse is also recognized as a form of domestic violence. This includes threats or intimidation, directed either at yourself or at your children. The following are examples of psychological abuse which may constitute domestic violence:

1. Your husband has been smoking crack cocaine, becomes angry, and threatens to kill you.

2. Your husband waves a knife in front of you and the kids, claiming he's going to "get rid of" anyone who doesn't do exactly as he says.

3. Your husband tells your children that he will burn down the house with them in it.

4. Although you have no source of income yourself, your husband refuses to give you money for food or medicine.

5. Your husband has locked you inside a bedroom or other room in the house and left you there for hours.

6. Your husband waved a gun or knife in your face, saying he was going to kill you, the kids, and himself. (Even if the gun is not loaded, this constitutes domestic violence.)

Remember, you don't need bruises or broken bones to prove that domestic violence has occurred.

I've Just Been Abused—Where Do I Turn?

If you have just experienced domestic violence, the first step is removing yourself and your children from the situation. Don't wait for your husband to strike out again. Leave the household immediately. Don't worry about taking clothes or other belongings. Just get out. If your husband won't let you leave, call the police or the emergency number, 911.

Once you have left, determine whether it is necessary to

obtain medical assistance. For legal and medical reasons, you should document the abuse that took place. An emergency-room report will provide a judge with the proof he needs when you ask that an Order of Protection be granted. Also, an injury might have occurred that isn't visible to the naked eye which requires treatment. Particularly if your children have been physically abused, be sure they see a doctor.

After obtaining medical help, go to the home of a friend or family member. If that is not possible, go to a shelter. Because domestic violence is so pervasive, many areas of the country now have battered women's shelters. These shelters will offer refuge to yourself and your children. The people at the shelter will not tell anyone that you are there, not even your husband, and they will offer you and your children a temporary place to stay, often free of charge. Most shelters keep a list of attorneys who work with victims of domestic violence and will refer you to such an attorney. Don't be too proud to accept the help that a shelter can provide.

If you need a shelter and don't know where one is located, call the local police, the emergency number (911), or the local hospital. Any of these sources will direct you to the nearest shelter in your area. Many divorce attorneys know of battered women's shelters in their area, so you may contact your lawyer for this information as well. Consult the listing in Appendix C for shelters in your area.

One last point about leaving home. Many women fear that if they leave their residence they will be charged with deser-tion. This is a myth. If you or your children have been the victims of domestic violence, not only can you leave but you and your children should leave immediately. You do not even have to tell your husband where you and your children have gone. Leaving your home under these circumstances does not constitute desertion.

Calling the Police

Once you have left the house, you must call the police and report the abuse that occurred. I realize that you fear retribution from your husband when he finds out. However, it is imperative that you report the abuse, not only for your immediate safety but for purposes of filing civil or criminal charges against him. This includes filing for your divorce. Many women begin divorce proceedings alleging that they have been abused for years. When asked for proof, though, there often isn't any documentation to back up these claims. Yet there are many ways to document the abuse:

- File a complaint or make out a police report.

- Seek medical treatment.

- Take photographs of your bruises or broken bones.

- Discuss the abuse with friends or family. (These people can testify for you or produce an affidavit to substantiate your claims.)

If you have failed to document the history of violence, the allegations you make during the divorce may amount to a situation of your word against his. While that doesn't mean your word won't be believed, the more evidence you have, the more success you will have in both your divorce case and other cases you may bring against your husband. Don't be victimized twice, first by your husband and then by the law. At the very least, fill out a criminal complaint against your husband. Even if you don't prosecute, the report will document the abuse that you or your children suffered.

Law enforcement regarding domestic violence has changed quite a bit in the last several years. Years ago women complained that the police would refuse to arrest the abuser, saying that it was "only a domestic disturbance." Today the law-enforcement community is well aware of the serious nature of domestic violence, and will not only arrest the husband but encourage the victim to prosecute him. Many police departments and state's attorney's offices have special divisions which deal only with crimes involving domestic violence. Such departments and offices often have victim's rights advocates, to support the victim both legally and emotionally while going through the legal process. If you are a victim of abuse, contact these offices and make use of their services. They are there to help you and your children. Let them, before it's too late.

Orders of Protection— Do They Really Work?

One of the first terms you are likely to hear in connection with domestic violence is "Order of Protection." You may have wondered what an Order of Protection is and how it could possibly protect you from an abusive husband. An Order of Protection, as its name implies, is a court order signed by a judge which restrains your husband from assaulting or threatening you or your children. (In some states, persons who are not married may obtain Orders of Protection. If you are a victim of abuse, but are not legally married to the abuser, contact a private attorney, the state's attorney's office or the local police for information about obtaining an appropriate Order of Protection.)

If you are married and the victim of abuse, you don't have to divorce your husband to obtain an Order of Protection. You can obtain an order through the criminal court even if you don't want to sue your husband for divorce. The state's attorney's office will act as your counsel, free of charge. You do not need a private attorney, but you may retain one if you wish.

To obtain a criminal Order of Protection, you must file a criminal complaint against your husband, asking that he be charged with abuse. Following his arrest, a hearing takes place to determine whether he is guilty of the claims you have made. At the hearing you must testify to the abuse that occurred and produce any evidence you may have of the abuse. If your husband is found guilty, he may be required to go to jail for a period of time. In almost all cases, though, the judge will enter an Order of Protection. The order will provide that your husband cannot come near you, assault you, harass or intimidate you. The same will apply to your children, if his behavior is found potentially dangerous to them. If your husband violates the Order of Protection, he could be sentenced to a lengthy period of time in jail.

If you are pursuing a divorce and you want an Order of

Protection entered, your lawyer will probably file a petition to obtain a civil Order of Protection. Frequently a petition for an Order of Protection is filed at the same time the petition for divorce is filed. The proceedings for a criminal and a civil Order of Protection are very similar. A major difference, however, is that a civil Order of Protection may be obtained ex parte— that is, without your husband having notice of the hearing or being present. Such an Order of Protection will be granted if the judge believes that giving your husband advance notice of the hearing would be likely to result in harm to yourself or your children. Again, you must testify at the hearing about the abuse and produce any relevant evidence. Generally, there is no rule requiring that the abuse take place within a limited number of days, months, or even years prior to the hearing. The order will be entered if the judge believes the violence happened and that you are now in reasonable fear for your safety and the safety of your children.

After the hearing, the sheriff will serve your husband with the Order of Protection (and the divorce papers, if those haven't been served before). If the Order of Protection was obtained without notice to your husband, the order will be in effect for only a few weeks. This is because the law gives your husband the right to come into court with a lawyer and tell his side of the story.

When the order expires, a full hearing will be held to determine whether a permanent order should be entered. Both you and your husband will have the opportunity to appear at that hearing and provide evidence. At the hearing on the permanent order, you must present documents or testimony in support of your allegations of abuse. Documentary evidence includes police reports, medical records, photographs, threatening notes, letters, or recordings made by your husband. Testimony can come from yourself and any other person who has knowledge of or witnessed the abuse. Generally, young children are not called to testify, but the judge may wish to speak with older children, such as teenagers.

One of three things will happen after the hearing. First, a permanent order may be entered with the consent of your husband. Second, the judge can enter an order which will remain in effect until the divorce is concluded. Third, the judge can refuse to enter a permanent order, concluding that you have not met your burden of proof.

Can I Kick My Husband Out of the House?

When your lawyer discusses the Order of Protection with you, she will ask whether you want the judge to order your husband to vacate the home, either temporarily or permanently. In most cases alleging abuse, lawyers ask that the husband be permanently removed from the residence, for the safety of the wife and the children.

To obtain an order permanently removing your husband from the household, you must usually demonstrate the following elements to the court:

a) that the abuse which you allege has occurred;

b) that further abuse is likely to occur;

c) that it would be a greater hardship for you and your children to leave than for your husband to leave;

d) that your husband has somewhere to go.

The last requirement might have taken you by surprise. After all, who cares where your husband lives, right? Well, in an era of economic hardship, men often come into court saying that they will be living on the streets if the judge kicks them out of the house. Remember, you are asking that your husband be required to find another place to live on a permanent basis. Unless you are presenting an extraordinarily serious case, a judge is not likely to force a man to live on the streets, if he truly has nowhere else to go.

If you want your husband removed from the home, either temporarily or permanently, you must be prepared when you go to court. Investigate whether your husband could stay with family, friends, or co-workers. If so, you may provide that information to the judge through your testimony, or you could present a statement signed by a third party saying that your husband has somewhere else to live for a period of time. If you give the judge options, he will be inclined to require that your husband leave the house. Obviously, the law prefers to err on the side of caution. The judge does not want you and your children back in a dangerous environment. You must help the court find the evidence necessary to rule in your favor.

What If My Husband Kidnaps the Children or Won't Give Them Back?

Abusive husbands sometimes threaten their wives with dire consequences if charges of abuse should ever be brought against them. One of the most common threats is that he will kidnap the children, or refuse to give the children back if he has physical possession of them. The subject of custody and kidnapping will be discussed in detail in Chapter 7. For now, let me briefly explain the relationship between temporary custody and an Order of Protection.

During the hearing on the Order of Protection, you may ask that the judge give you temporary custody of your children, due to threats of kidnapping or other harm against your children by your husband. At this stage of the proceeding, a judge cannot grant you permanent custody. An order of permanent custody can only be entered when your divorce becomes final. However, the judge can restrict your husband's right to be with the children and can award you temporary custody, based upon the evidence presented at the hearing on the Order of Protection. In fact, even if you left your children in the physical possession of your husband, the judge can require that your husband turn the children over to you, based upon threats which your husband has made or other inappropriate behavior he has exhibited.

The law regarding custody differs from state to state, so you should speak with an attorney in your area about specific questions you have involving custody and kidnapping.

If I Prove My Husband Is Abusive, Does It Mean I'll Get Everything in the Divorce?

This is a very common question. Again, while the law differs from state to state, the general answer is no. In many states, your husband's abusive conduct is absolutely irrelevant to a distribution of property. As a result, you should not automatically assume that if your husband has been found guilty of abuse, you'll walk away with the lion's share of the assets.

In some ways, however, your husband's behavior may be very relevant, and may indirectly lead to a greater distribution to you. For example, if the court is convinced that your spouse won't pay you court-ordered maintenance (alimony), the judge may grant you a greater percentage of the marital estate. If it appears that your husband won't pay child support, the court may require that certain assets which would have been awarded to him be held in escrow, to allow for payments relating to child support or the cost of educational or medical expenses.

Of course, your husband's behavior may cause the judge to restrict your husband's rights to custody of or visitation with the children. If you are particularly concerned about this issue, you should be very motivated to file charges against your husband for his abusive behavior. Depending on the nature and severity of his prior actions, the judge may order that you be granted sole custody of the children and that your husband have only limited visitation with the children. Your husband may be allowed to see the children very rarely or when his visits are supervised by a third party.

In short, your husband's abusive behavior may result in a settlement which is more favorable for you and, more importantly, may result in a restriction of his rights to custody and visitation.

Stalking

Last year one of the first anti-stalking laws in the nation was passed in Illinois. This new law recognizes stalking as a form of domestic violence. Historically, it was very difficult to prosecute a defendant for stalking unless some type of physical abuse accompanied his stalking. Media attention has helped us see that victims of stalking are subjected to conduct which can be physically dangerous and emotionally devastating.

Years ago the law-enforcement community was less sensitive to the problem we now call stalking. It was often believed that women were simply exaggerating the advances of a man who had cared for them or that she was somehow encouraging his behavior—leading him on. Some even suggested that women should be appreciative of continued male advances. Thankfully, stalking is now recognized for the crime that it is, and complaints by victims are taken seriously.

Research shows that almost all cases of stalking involve people who know one another and that most are former love interests or persons now divorced from each other. Stalking usually begins when the victim ends a relationship with the stalker. Experts believe that stalkers have a need for power and control over the victim, much like rapists and other perpetrators of violence against women.

To prove that you are a victim of stalking, you must show that the defendant threatened you and followed you or placed you under surveillance. Generally, a threat is any action which reasonably causes you to fear being harmed or assaulted. Typical conduct by stalkers includes following victims to their place of employment, making harassing phone calls, and sending threatening letters. In extreme cases, victims have had their tires slashed, had dead animals deposited on their doorsteps, and have been physically attacked by the stalker.

Hopefully, every other state will follow Illinois and legally recognize stalking as a form of domestic violence and, like Illinois, make the crime punishable by many years in the penitentiary.

The Worst Thing to Do Is Nothing

We know that a great number of men in our society have serious problems involving violent and abusive behavior toward women and children. Abuse won't necessarily stop just because legal papers are served on your husband. An Order of Protection can't stop a bullet. You can't control your husband or his actions, but you can take control of the situation.

If you or your children are victims of domestic violence, get out. Talk about what has been happening, whether to friends, family, or co-workers. Don't keep the violence a secret. Contact a lawyer or the police about filing civil or criminal charges against your husband. Legally, emotionally, and physically, the sooner you act, the better off you and your children will be.

Chapter 5

Filing for Divorce—
Strategies and
Considerations

What do you do when you've decided to proceed with the divorce? Contrary to what many women have been led to believe, it's not as simple as breaking the bad news to one's spouse and filing the necessary papers. How and when you file and break the bad news can have tremendous legal ramifications for you and your children. Mistakes are easily made in the highly emotional few weeks after women finally decide to get divorces. Let's examine the preventative measures you can take to avoid these mistakes and put yourself and your children in a strong legal position.

Should I tell my husband that I'm going to divorce him?

You might think this is an odd question. After all, by the time someone visits a divorce lawyer, the subject of divorce must have been discussed once or twice, right? I have found that often this is not the case. Even in marriages that have been troubled for many years, the subject of divorce may never have been discussed. In other marriages, though, getting a divorce may be discussed on a daily basis. In either situation, the actual filing for divorce may come as a great shock to your spouse.

You may be surprised to learn that the law does not require you to notify your husband before you file for divorce; it only requires that your husband receive copies of the divorce papers after they have been filed. Many husbands don't learn of the divorce until the sheriff serves them with divorce papers. Deciding whether to tell your spouse about the divorce before he is served is both a legal and an emotional issue. Although you may wish to tell him, your lawyer may counsel against it. This is because giving your spouse prior notice of the divorce may place you at physical or financial risk.

For example, if you fear that your husband might react violently to the news of the divorce, you don't want to be the person communicating this information. In this situation I recommend that you say nothing about the divorce until the sheriff serves the papers on your husband. You and your children shouldn't even be present when your husband first learns of the divorce. Your lawyer should arrange service of the papers so that you and your children can leave the home before the sheriff arrives.

If you believe your husband might stop paying the bills, say nothing about the divorce until the mortgage and utilities have been fully paid for the month. I certainly wouldn't want your husband to be served with the papers the day before the rent is due or before he has given you the grocery money for the month.

In deciding whether to tell your husband, you must determine whether giving him advance notice of the divorce will benefit you in both the short run and the long term. As you can see, there are many good reasons not to discuss the divorce before the papers have been served. If you know the divorce will not be amicable and that you will have to fight with him every step of the way, don't tell him ahead of time about filing for divorce. Let him find out from the sheriff. On the other hand, proceeding in this fashion may unnecessarily increase the bad feelings between you and your husband and cause him to be spiteful as a result of your failure to tell him yourself. For many men, having a sheriff come to their place of business to serve divorce papers is the ultimate humiliation. You don't want to turn a relatively amicable situation into World War III.

If you and your spouse have talked openly about the divorce, and you do not fear physical or financial repercussions, telling him you've decided to file may be most beneficial to you in the long run. Remember the saying "You get more with honey than you do with vinegar." Appearing to be cooperative may be in your best interests. Let me give you an idea of how to approach your husband so that he believes you are really working in his interest.

Choose an appropriate time to sit down with him and discuss the decision you've made to proceed with the divorce. Tell him that you have advised your lawyer that you wish to make things as easy on him as possible. Let him know that you want to be very cooperative and work with him in amicably resolving the situation. Tell him that, to show your good faith, you convinced your lawyer not to have the sheriff serve the divorce papers on him at work. Advise him that if he agrees to accept the papers from your lawyer directly and signs a statement saying that he will submit to the jurisdiction of the court, there is no need for the sheriff to serve the papers. Check with your lawyer to make sure your state allows this alternative to service by the sheriff.

Saving your husband the embarrassment of having the sheriff appear at his place of business can go a long way toward negotiating an advantageous settlement and resolving the divorce quickly. However, this olive branch should only be extended if your lawyer determines that doing so would be in your best interests. Maintaining a civilized relationship and talking to your husband directly is the method most lawyers prefer, providing it does not place you in jeopardy. Believe it or not, attorneys generally encourage an amicable resolution to the divorce. Usually, the news of a divorce best comes directly from you, as opposed to your lawyer or the sheriff.

You may be saying to yourself, "I want my husband to know I've decided to file for divorce, but I just can't bring myself to tell him." Many women are not comfortable with the idea of confronting their husbands with the decision to get a divorce. For some, the experience is too emotionally difficult. If you can't tell your husband face to face that you want a divorce, but don't want the news to come from the sheriff, consider the following options.

• Put it in writing

You may find it easier to tell him about your decision in writing. Write a heartfelt letter to your husband, telling him about your feelings and why you have made the decision to pursue a divorce. For some women, writing the letter can be a cathartic experience. It may not only provide a practical way to tell your husband but also help you deal with the divorce on an emotional level. Have your lawyer review the letter first, before giving it to your husband. You may have been quite emotional when you wrote it and might have made statements and admissions against your own interests.

- Have your lawyer tell him

Another option is to have your lawyer tell your husband. This option should only be pursued if your situation is very amicable but you cannot bring yourself to tell your spouse yourself. If this is the case, your lawyer will inform your spouse that the divorce papers have been filed and ask whether he intends to cooperate amicably in the divorce process. Talk to your attorney about whether she would feel comfortable conveying this information and whether she believes it would be in your best interests.

I'm afraid my husband will steal or destroy our possessions when he finds out.

This very common fear is, unfortunately, all too well founded. It is not unusual for an angry spouse to "clean out the house" when he learns of the divorce, taking everything that isn't nailed down. After removing certain items, he may even claim that many possessions never really existed. There are several preventative measures you can take if you fear this might happen.

1. Take photographs of your possessions before your husband learns of the divorce, and give your attorney the photographs for safekeeping. If possible, make a videotape of all your possessions, just as you would for insurance purposes. Give the tape to your lawyer.

2. Make a detailed inventory of the items in your home. The inventory should include everything, from your furniture and furnishings to your clothing and jewelry. Don't forget to list the children's clothing and toys. Give the list to your lawyer before your husband learns of the divorce.

3. Gather any receipts, charge-card statements, or other documents to prove the existence of as many possessions as possible and to prove their value. Give these documents to your attorney before your husband learns of the divorce.

4. Remove particular items that have the greatest sentimental or actual cash value before your husband learns of the divorce. Place them with friends, with family, or in storage for safekeeping.

5. Have at least one witness with you when your husband returns to the home after he first learns of the divorce. If possessions are going to be destroyed, it usually happens in the heat of the moment right after your spouse finds out about the divorce. A witness will provide some safety for you and your possessions. In more extreme cases, consider having a police officer present.

6. Make sure you have a current, paid-up insurance policy covering the present cash value of your possessions and make sure the policy covers accidental breakage.

As we all know, divorce can cause people to temporarily lash out. Possessions may be destroyed in the aftermath of receiving the bad news, or deliberately, after much time has passed. I have seen cases where valuable objects were purposefully destroyed, just to get back at the other party. In one case the husband ruined all of his wife's designer clothing by dumping her Givenchy and St. Laurent on the front lawn, rolling over them with a lawnmower and then turning the hose on them. In another case the husband took a sledgehammer and smashed the antique figures of children that his wife spent twenty-five years collecting.

Remember the movie *The War of the Roses*? You may not think it could happen, but your spouse may lose control and destroy some of your most treasured items. Follow the steps listed above to safeguard your possessions.

Why does the sheriff have to serve the papers on my husband?

After your lawyer has filed your divorce papers at the courthouse, the sheriff must personally serve your husband with the papers (unless your spouse agreed to accept them from your attorney). In either situation, once your husband receives the papers, your case can proceed and you can get a divorce—even if your husband never shows up in court.

Some husbands are determined to "evade service." They figure that if they don't accept the papers, they can prevent you from getting a divorce. We will discuss later why this is not true. However, there are other legal reasons why it is more advantageous for your husband to be served with the papers and why this step is important to your case.

If your husband is evading service, the sheriff may have a difficult time serving the papers on him. For example, if your husband refuses to open the door for the sheriff, the papers can't be personally served. If your husband's employer refuses to allow the sheriff onto business premises, it may be impossible for the sheriff to actually serve the papers.

In situations where the sheriff has not been successful in personally serving the documents on your husband, a private process server can be hired. Most states allow a private person to serve the documents only after the sheriff has first tried and been unsuccessful. A private process server is any person of legal age who is not a party to your case. Therefore, neither you nor your children could be appointed special process servers in your divorce case.

Process servers must be very creative to successfully serve the legal documents, since they know the defendant is trying to avoid service. People who work as process servers are often the last ones you'd think would have such a job, which is why they make good process servers—they don't look official. Unlike sheriffs, they don't wear a uniform, so the defendant has no advance warning when he is approached.

When I was in school, I worked as a law clerk at a law firm. One of the first jobs I had was to act as a process server and try to serve a doctor whom we were suing for malpractice. Dr. "Smith" had evaded service for months, always claiming that he was either seeing a patient or in surgery. I developed a plan I thought could work. I made an appointment to see Dr. Smith, saying I was a new patient. When I arrived at his office, the nurse put me in an examining room, told me to remove my clothing, and said that Dr. Smith would be with me shortly. The door to the examining room opened and Dr. Smith walked in. When he asked why I wasn't undressed, I handed him the papers and dashed for the door.

Don't be scared by your husband's antics. In almost all cases a private process server will be able to track down your husband and serve him. Even if it means dressing up as a deliveryman and handing your husband a pizza box with the papers inside, process servers usually "get their man."

If my husband just takes off, can I still get a divorce?

You will be happy to know that even if your husband did actually disappear, you could still get a divorce. The law does not require that you stay married to him forever, even if you can't find him. However, you might be able to get only a divorce, not child support or maintenance.

All states provide that, in order to divorce your husband, you must first have obtained proper service on him. Unless you obtain proper service, you will not be granted a divorce. We have already discussed the most common way of serving your husband, which is by having a sheriff or special process server personally deliver the documents to him. In some states personal service also includes serving the papers on a member of your husband's household.

If your husband has successfully avoided service, or if he has disappeared and you aren't sure where he is, you can still "serve" him and get your divorce. How? Service by publication is your answer. You have probably seen the legal notices that appear in newspapers. These notices inform persons who cannot be located that legal proceedings have been filed which may affect their rights. Most states provide that service by publication is an acceptable way of informing your husband of the divorce, if every other avenue has been pursued.

Once your husband has been served, or the publication has appeared, your husband will have a limited period of time to obtain a lawyer and file papers with the court. In most states, the period of time is approximately thirty days. If he does nothing, you may appear before the judge and obtain a divorce without your husband being present.

However, when you obtain a divorce without your husband being present, the court can only award you a Default Judgment of Divorce. This means that your husband was in default for his failure to appear before the court. While the court may legally grant your divorce, it may not have the power to deal with property or financial issues, such as alimony or child support. Therefore, if your husband is not present, the judge may grant the divorce itself, but may have to grant you the right to come back into court in the future and request that your husband pay alimony or child support if he can be found or if property which he owns can be located.

Will my husband have to pay the bills after I file for divorce?

While your husband may not physically disappear when he learns of the divorce, his financial support may vanish. I've found that many men react to the news by refusing to pay bills or give their wives any money. You can and should file a motion with the court asking that your husband be required to contribute to the running of the household. However, obtaining that order usually takes two months or longer. Until then, you need to take the following measures to ensure your survival during the weeks or months ahead.

1. Establish a financial plan that's designed to keep your head above water for a three-month period.

2. Follow my earlier advice about timing the arrival of the divorce papers so they arrive after major bills have been paid.

3. Withdraw money from joint accounts and deposit money in an account in your name. Check with your lawyer first, since each state handles this issue differently. In most states, however, you can use this money for such things as food, medicine, and housing. You can't use it for a new mink coat or an Aruba vacation—and you'll have to account to the court for the money you withdrew and repay money that wasn't spent on necessities.

4. Establish and use credit. If you don't have sufficient savings to carry you through the next few months, take a cash advance on your charge card. Again, money spent on necessities probably won't have to be reimbursed. If you don't have a charge card in your name, apply for one. Many women find it difficult to obtain credit after the divorce, especially if they don't have high-paying jobs.

My husband says he'll drag this case on for years. What happens in the meantime?

Women are often shocked to learn that it may take years before their case is resolved. Husbands delay, court calendars are filled, and time drags on. In the meantime, someone must pay the mortgage, utilities, and other monthly bills. After all, you certainly can't keep borrowing money from friends or taking cash advances to keep up with expenses. In addition, a decision must be made about whether your husband is going to continue living in the house or whether he will move.

Regardless of where your husband will live, bills must be paid. If you and your husband cannot come to an agreement about this issue, it will eventually be decided by a judge. A hearing will be held to determine the necessary expenses and the income presently available to meet those expenses. If your husband has moved and his income isn't enough to support two households, the judge may require that you go to work immediately to provide more income. The judge will enter an order stating who is responsible for paying particular bills, and this order will continue until the divorce is final or until the circumstances change and another hearing is held.

When deciding whether you want your husband to leave the house, you should first determine whether his income will be sufficient to pay for two households. If it is not, you may wish to rethink the importance of his leaving immediately. Women often assume, incorrectly, that their husband will automatically leave the house after the divorce has gotten underway. However, unless you obtained an Order of Protection requiring that he leave (see Chapter 4), your husband may remain in the house until the divorce is final, even if you object. While it used to be common for husbands to move, these days it is less likely that your husband will do so. His lawyer may specifically advise him not to move out, especially if they know you want him to leave. His lawyer hopes that the situation will be so unpleasant that you'll do anything to get him out—even if it means entering into a fast settlement that is unfair to you.

In some cases, however, your husband may be advised to leave the home and move into his own place. If he establishes a separate residence, your husband will then have expenses that probably cannot be supported by his salary alone. If so, the judge is more likely to require that you go back to work to help support the household or to sell the house because there is insufficient income to pay the expenses.

Whether your husband is unwilling or unable to provide for two households, chances are you will join the growing number of couples who live under the same roof while going through a divorce. This situation may exist for months or even years, until your divorce is final. I have seen situations where couples divide the house down the middle, with each party having rights to separate areas. There are many cases where the husband lives in the basement or on another floor, while his wife and children remain on a separate level of the home. This can be an emotionally draining situation for everyone.

Prior to filing for divorce, ask yourself whether you want your husband to stay in the home so the bills can be paid, or whether you could continue to live in your home and pay the necessary bills with little help from your husband. Answer the following questions, often asked by judges in financial hearings, to determine what is financially possible and to assess how much you can expect your husband to contribute financially, regardless of where he lives.

Will you and your husband continue to live in the same household or will he be living separately?

If your husband moves, will he stay with family or friends rent-free? If not, about how much will he pay in rent? What additional expenses will there be if your husband moves? For example, will you have to buy a second car?

Do you and your husband make enough money every month to pay the current bills? If not, it is almost certain that you will have to go back to work, especially if he decides to move out, or sell the house.

Are you employed on a full-time basis? Would your salary alone cover the current household bills? Think of the worst-case scenario—if your husband moves and pays you nothing, regardless of a court order, would you be able to stay? If not, consider the possibility of moving (but first see Chapter 6).

If you must return to work, what salary can you expect and what is the cost of day care?

If you rent, is your name on the lease or his? If his name is the only one, perhaps you should move and let him keep the apartment and assume responsibility for the rent.

Can you get a loan from friends, family, or a commercial lending institution to help you with the bills on a temporary basis?

Appendix A contains a form called an income and expense affidavit. Complete this form and use it to compare current or projected income with expenses. It will help you determine how much you'll need for basic bills, whether it would be financially best for your husband to stay or move, and whether there will be sufficient income to allow you and the children to stay in the house.

Unfortunately, it's not a question of what's fair. It's a question of what is affordable.

SECTION · II

Chapter 6

Getting What You Want and Not What He Wants You to Have

One of the first questions asked of divorce lawyers is: "What kind of property settlement can I expect to receive?" To answer this question, your lawyer must have a complete understanding of your finances, including all assets and debts. Unfortunately, this is an area where women are often at a loss. Many women are unable to answer questions regarding finances because they do not possess this information themselves. This happens more commonly than is often thought. When I ask a client for basic financial information, it is not unusual for her to say, "You'll think I'm really dumb, but I have no idea how much money my husband makes," or "I'm very embarrassed to admit this, but I don't know exactly how much money we have in the bank." When I request an itemization of the monthly expenses, she tells me that her husband pays the bills.

Without a clear picture of your assets and debts you will

never be able to reach a fair settlement; nor will you have the information necessary to begin planning for your life after the divorce. Do you know what property is legally considered "yours"? Are you aware that your lawyer can use the power of the court to uncover assets that your husband has hidden? We will review the steps that will allow you to reach a property settlement agreement that is fair to you and your children.

Step 1: Yours, Mine, and Ours. Marital vs. Nonmarital Property

After Jack married Lynda, he received a large bonus check and purchased an expensive stereo system for himself. Lynda has never used these items. When Jack divorces Lynda, will she have any claim to the stereo system?

During their marriage, Mark's paycheck was always deposited into his own checking account. When Nancy files for divorce, is she entitled to anything in that account?

I have found that the greatest misconception people have about divorces involves the subject of dividing up property. The fact is, people usually don't realize who owns what. As a result, spouses often believe they are entitled to particular items of property, when, in fact, they have absolutely no legal rights to that property. It is imperative that you understand which assets you are legally entitled to, since the divorce court cannot grant you property to which you have no legal claim.

In the examples above, do you think Lynda has rights in Jack's stereo system? Should Nancy receive some portion of the checking account? In most states, the answer to these questions would be yes, since the stereo system and the bank account are both considered marital property. This means that both spouses own these items and the court can divide them any way it sees fit. In many states the court could award the entire stereo system to Lynda and all the money in the bank account to Nancy. As a general rule, the law considers all items acquired after the marriage to be marital property.

It is imperative that you understand the difference between marital and nonmarital property, for two reasons. First, you can make a claim only to what is considered marital property. Nonmarital property is off-limits. Second, in many states the court is not required to divide marital property fifty-fifty, but can divide it in some other percentage, depending upon the facts and circumstances of each case. There are a few states which have community-property laws rather than marital-property laws. Community-property states require that all property acquired during the marriage must be divided equally, unless a prenuptial agreement provides otherwise. In states that follow marital-property laws, marital assets and marital debts may be divided in any percentage the court finds equitable. The community-property states are Arizona, California, Idaho, Louisiana, Nevada, New Mexico, Texas, Washington, and Wisconsin.

If you live in a state that follows the laws of marital property, as opposed to community property, income earned during the marriage by you and your husband is considered marital property. This is why the stereo purchased by Jack is as much Lynda's as it is his. Since earned income is marital property, employment benefits earned during the marriage are also considered marital property. For example, if your husband participates in a pension or profit-sharing plan, you are entitled to a percentage of these benefits even though they have been earned as a result of his employment.

At this point you are probably wondering, "If my husband and I both own the stereo, what about the jewelry and fur coat he gave me during our marriage? Are those things mine?" The answer, in most states, is that you are 100 percent entitled to those items because gifts are usually an exception to the rule of marital property. Gifts are considered nonmarital and, therefore, not subject to division by the divorce court. Any items that are considered nonmarital must be distributed to the party who originally owned the item. This same exception usually applies to property that has been inherited and has remained nonmarital. For example, if your aunt died and left you $10,000, that money is nonmarital. However, some states provide that you can transform the money into marital property. If you use the money to buy furniture and furnishings for the house, go on vacation with your husband, or pay the mortgage, you may have changed part or all of the funds into marital property. If you do receive inherited property and wish it to remain nonmarital, it is best to keep the funds in an account in your name only and not spend the money on items related to the marriage.

Another example of nonmarital property, to which you have no claim, are items obtained prior to the marriage. If your husband owned that stereo before you were married, in most states it would be considered his nonmarital property and must be returned to him during the divorce. In that situation, you would have no claim to the stereo. As a general rule, each party is entitled to keep any items they owned prior to the marriage.

As you can see, property acquired during the marriage is

usually considered marital. You may make a claim on any marital items that you wish and the court can divide the marital property in a way it deems just and equitable. Nonmarital items, on the other hand, cannot be divided by the court and must be distributed to the party who brought the item into the marriage. Now that you have an idea of what types of items may constitute marital and nonmarital property, your next step is locating all the assets and determining the extent of the debts. This will be done during the discovery phase of the litigation.

Step 2: The Discovery Phase (Locating Assets and Debts)

We have all heard the horror stories of divorce cases that have taken years to resolve. Cases often take so long to wind their way through the legal process because of what is called the discovery phase of the litigation. In this part of the case each party has the right to conduct an investigation regarding marital and nonmarital property and learn any other information that may be relevant to the case.

Completing discovery is not necessarily essential in every divorce case. If you truly believe that you are aware of all of the assets and debts that exist, you might decide to instruct your attorney to waive discovery. However, most people usually participate in some amount of discovery, just to make sure that all the assets and debts have been disclosed. There are many avenues of investigation your lawyer can use to obtain financial information necessary to resolve your case. The two most com-

mon methods of investigation are through depositions and subpoenas.

Depositions

The most basic type of discovery conducted by your lawyer
involves the taking of depositions. In a deposition, a person
(called the deponent) gives testimony under oath. Anyone who
may have information relevant to your case can be deposed. Of
course, the first people to be deposed will be you and your
husband. Your lawyer will take your husband's deposition and
your husband's lawyer will take yours. Each deposition can last
an hour, a day, or a week, depending upon how much information must be obtained. Commonly, they last less than one day.

Although depositions are taken in attorney's offices, the
testimony given is legally equivalent to testifying in court at
trial. Every word that is said is recorded by a court reporter and
is made part of the court transcript. During a deposition, the
lawyer has free rein to ask questions of the witness and to
demand that those questions be answered. As a party to the
case, you have a right to be present at the depositions. However, it is usually recommended that both parties not be present, since your husband and other deponents may make statements or allegations with which you take issue. It can be an
emotionally draining experience and it is best left to your lawyer to handle.

The deposition is an important part of your case, and lawyers spend a great deal of time preparing their clients for giving
testimony. This is done not only to refresh your recollection of

certain facts but also because the opposing lawyer, in addition to wanting information from you, may want to make you look bad. There are many different styles that lawyers use in taking depositions. Some lawyers try to scare you, others try to be your best friend. I often tell clients the following story to illustrate that testifying at a deposition can be very tricky.

Several years ago I was preparing to take the deposition of "Mr. Diamond," a businessman who owned many different companies. Some of these businesses were quite complex, and I was unfamiliar with the industry in which the businesses operated. I was very concerned about this deposition, especially since I knew that Mr. Diamond did not want to be deposed and his lawyer would spend hours coaching him. However, I needed to understand how his businesses operated and I knew that Mr. Diamond was the only person who could supply that information.

On the day of the deposition I introduced myself to Mr. Diamond, a man in his late fifties. It was clear that Mr. Diamond would have preferred undergoing a root canal to being deposed. I advised Mr. Diamond, his lawyer, and the court reporter that I wanted to make a statement to the deponent before taking the deposition. I told Mr. Diamond that I had spent many hours preparing for his deposition, and that it was obvious that he was an intelligent, successful businessman who certainly couldn't be tripped up by my simple questions. I assured him that I had no hidden agenda and that my only purpose was to learn about his businesses. Finally, I said that I was aware of how valuable his time was and that I would try to complete the deposition as soon as possible. However, his businesses were quite involved and it might take me a very long time to depose him, unless he made every effort to help me understand how the businesses operated.

Mr. Diamond spent hours educating me about his companies, much to the dismay of his lawyer, who had spent a great deal of time coaching him not to cooperate with me. Yet I was able to undo all of his advance preparation with a "sincere" five-minute discussion. Don't be fooled, like Mr. Diamond, into thinking the opposing lawyer is your friend and that we're really "all on the same side." There are many pitfalls to avoid in giving your deposition. When it's time for you to give your deposition, remember the following rules:

1. Don't volunteer information. Answer only the question you're asked.

Everyone has skeletons in their closets. It is the job of the opposing attorney to find those skeletons, no matter how small they may be, and use them to the advantage of his client. The less you say, the better the chances that the skeletons will stay where they belong.

2. Never state facts you don't know.

You are better off saying "I don't know" a thousand times than assuming or making up facts, however innocently. If your husband's attorney can show that you lied or made something up, even once, he's accomplished his mission. He can use that one falsehood again and again to show the court that you are not credible and cannot be trusted. If that is done, the judge is legally allowed to dismiss many other parts of your testimony on the basis of lack of credibility.

3. Don't argue or become emotional with the lawyer.

State your answers calmly and reasonably. When people become upset, they are more likely to blurt out statements that turn out to be more harmful to them than to the other side. You don't want your husband portraying you as a hysterical woman, causing the judge to question your rationality. It is the job of your lawyer to argue; it is neither necessary nor wise for you to do so with the other lawyer.

4. Don't chat with the opposing lawyer, court reporter, or office staff during a break or after the deposition.

You'd be amazed at how much lawyers learn this way. Remember, your husband's lawyer is trying to find any information that he can use against you. The simplest things can be twisted and misunderstood. Confine your discussion to talking about the weather and not much more.

5. If you don't understand a question, ask that it be rephrased.

Never answer a question you don't understand. Far too often clients think they know what the lawyer is trying to get at and begin shooting from the hip in an effort to answer the question they think was asked. Lawyers often find out information because the deponent misunderstood the question and provided information in an area the lawyer hadn't even considered. If there is any doubt that the question could be taken more than one way, ask that it be clarified.

6. Tell the truth.

You can explain the truth but you can never explain a lie. If you know that topics will be brought up that you are uncomfortable with, speak with your attorney before the deposition. While you should never lie, you may be able to explain the situation in a way that is less damaging to you.

Subpoenas

Another method of investigation which your lawyer may use involves the subpoena power of the court. Lawyers can require the production of any documentation that may be relevant to your case. In most divorce cases, the documents requested will relate to the finances, such as income, expenses, assets, and debts. Spouses are commonly asked to produce documents such as bank statements and income-tax returns. However, any type of document may be obtained, including medical records. For example, if your husband claims he cannot work because of an injury, your lawyer will ask that he produce his medical records or any other information that could be relevant to this issue. If there are disputes regarding custody or visitation, any documents that could impact on decisions regarding the children may be requested.

If your husband refuses to voluntarily produce documents

that have been requested, your lawyer can subpoena the documents from the party who has custody of the records. For example, your lawyer can directly subpoena banks, stockbrokers, and accountants. We frequently subpoena the records of the husband's employer to confirm the amount of income the husband receives and the type of benefits to which he is entitled. Anyone who has documentation relevant to the proceedings may be subpoenaed and required to produce this information. If they refuse to do so, a court may require them to produce the records and hold the party in contempt for failing to comply with the court's order.

Must I go through the discovery process? Can I waive my rights and just get the divorce over with?

The discovery process can be extremely time-consuming and expensive. If you figure out the time it would take to locate every document relating to all the assets and debts acquired since the first day of your marriage, and then estimate how long it would take your lawyer to review these documents, it's easy to see why the discovery phase of your case could take months or even years to complete.

However, you may decide that going through discovery is not necessary in your situation. If you have handled the family finances and are fully aware of all the relevant financial information, you may decide to waive your rights to discovery. Remember, the purpose of discovery is to disclose all necessary information, primarily financial. If you have all the facts needed to make an informed decision about settlement, you could save yourself a great deal of time and money by waiving discovery. If you do choose to waive your discovery rights, your lawyer will ask you to sign a release stating that you have been informed of your legal right to discovery and you have decided not to pursue that option.

I urge you to be very cautious about waiving your rights to discovery. More than one client has said, "I know what assets there are to divide; my husband isn't hiding anything. Besides, it will cost me more money and delay my divorce." Then six months later she finds out her former husband bought his girlfriend a fur coat, although she thought he was broke. If you decide to waive your discovery rights, follow these steps:

1. Have your attorney draft an inventory of all assets that currently exist and have that inventory signed by your husband. The inventory should also state that there are no other assets that haven't been disclosed.

2. Include a provision in the final settlement agreement which states that if, in the future, you should find that your husband did not disclose all assets, you will automatically be entitled to 50 percent of the undisclosed assets (or more), plus any attorney's fees necessary for you to collect.

In most cases, some discovery must be conducted to provide the information necessary to obtain the best settlement agreement for you and your children. Discuss discovery with your attorney to determine how extensive the process should be.

Step 3: The Final Settlement Agreement

When the discovery phase of the litigation has been completed, you will have a list of the marital assets and debts available for distribution and a knowledge of what items are arguably nonmarital. The question becomes: What is a fair settlement for you and your children? To answer that question you must consider numerous issues. For example, who should receive the real estate, furniture, and other property items, such as the bank accounts and automobiles? You must determine whether you are a candidate for spousal support, and if so, how much should be paid and for how long? Finally, you must consider how to handle the division of retirement benefits and the tax ramifications of the settlement.

Naturally, your lawyer will counsel you on these issues as they relate to your case. Since over 90 percent of all divorce cases end up settling rather than going to trial, the probability is very high that your case will be settled. In order to reach a fair settlement, however, you must be aware of the major issues that affect you. The following discussion will highlight the most important financial issues relating to property settlement agreements.

Spousal support. How much and for how long?

Spousal support, also referred to as spousal maintenance, is the current term for what we used to call alimony. We've all heard those old jokes about the husband who had to pay alimony for the rest of his life after being married only six months. Johnny Carson would remind us practically every night that he had to keep working so his former wives could receive their alimony payments. How often do you think women are awarded alimony? Ninety percent of the time? Seventy percent of the time? Perhaps half of the time?

The fact is, women receive alimony in less than 15 percent of all divorce cases. Worse yet, if you are one of the lucky few to get maintenance, you will be shocked by the low amount and the brief period of time that you will receive maintenance. It will also come as a major surprise that maintenance, unlike child support, is taxable to you. It is imperative that you be realistic in assessing your chances of obtaining maintenance and the amount you will require to meet your living expenses, considering the taxes you'll be paying. If it doesn't appear likely that you will receive support, you will have to reconsider the remainder of the divorce settlement and determine how much of the total assets you must ask for to compensate you for the lack of maintenance. Of course, the law regarding spousal support varies from state to state, so you must discuss this issue in depth with your lawyer.

As a general rule, in order to obtain spousal support you must prove two things. First, you must show that you are unable to meet your financial needs based upon your current ability to earn income. Second, you must demonstrate that your spouse has the ability to pay maintenance. This may seem simple, but the determination of whether you are entitled to support is a very complicated matter.

Take the case of David and Anne. They were married for seven years and had two children, ages five and three. Anne worked as a schoolteacher before the birth of their first child; since then she has been a full-time homemaker. David has worked as a mechanic for the last ten years. Anne filed for divorce six months ago and wonders if she is a candidate for maintenance. Do you think the court will award Anne maintenance?

Not likely. David probably doesn't make enough money to allow Anne to stay at home after the divorce, since he doesn't have enough income to support two households. As a result, Anne will not be able to remain at home until her children reach school age, even though this is the arrangement that she and David agreed upon during the marriage. Anne will have to put her children in day care and go back to working full-time as a teacher. She will probably receive child support from David but no maintenance.

David and Anne's case is typical. After the divorce, Anne will have to pay the expenses of day care and support the children out of her income and the child support that, hopefully, she receives from David. No wonder most women and children have a reduced standard of living after a divorce, whereas men enjoy a better standard of living. The inability to receive maintenance is one of the reasons for this inequality.

Remember that even if you can prove the need for maintenance, you must show that your husband has the ability to pay. Obviously, if you and your husband were barely making ends meet, it is unrealistic to expect that you will receive maintenance after the divorce is final. In deciding whether you are entitled to maintenance, the judge looks at the financial circumstances that exist at the time of the divorce. If your husband has just lost his job or didn't get that promotion he's been waiting for, you might want to put the divorce on hold. Some people decide not to file for divorce until their financial situation improves.

Don't be fooled, though, if your husband's financial circumstances suddenly take a downturn just after you file for divorce. Did your husband coincidentally lose his job shortly after you served him with the divorce papers? If so, you are not alone. Some men will do anything to avoid paying their wives maintenance, even if it means sabotaging their own careers. Was your husband's sudden job loss a coincidence or could it have been planned? Don't become guilt-ridden, believing that filing for divorce set off a series of terrible events, leaving your husband in the depths of despair. I have seen women enter into quick settlement agreements, giving up everything, because their husbands made it appear that things had fallen apart since the divorce papers were filed. If your husband "suddenly" suffers financial reversals, allow your lawyer to use the subpoena and deposition powers of the court to determine whether your husband is playing financial games. Remember, his income is a marital asset. You have a right to know why that asset no longer exists or why it has been diminished.

You may be asking yourself, "Will the court *ever* award maintenance?" There are situations in which it is more likely that the court will award maintenance. For example, if your husband is wealthy and your income is minimal, the judge is likely to award you maintenance to correct the disparity in income that exists between you and your husband. Furthermore, if your husband earned a substantial income, a court will consider your high standard of living in setting a maintenance award.

Other situations that increase your chances of receiving support include long-term marriages of at least ten years or more and cases in which the wife has no marketable skills sufficient to allow her to earn a living wage. Also, if a physical disability prevents you from working or you have a child with a physical disability, the court may have no other option but to grant you maintenance, on either a short-term or long-term basis.

In determining whether you are entitled to support, the court will consider many factors, such as:

- The length of the marriage

- Your educational background

- The number of children in the household and whether they have any physical or emotional disabilities

- Your physical and emotional health

- The standard of living you enjoyed during the marriage

- Your current ability to earn income

- Your husband's ability to earn income

- The net value of the assets you will receive in the divorce

You might be surprised by the last item. The judge is likely to consider the assets you'll receive in the divorce settlement. If you receive a substantial asset, such as the house or a large bank account, the judge might refuse to grant you spousal support, on the basis that you could sell the asset and have a great deal of money on which to live. This comes as a great surprise to most women, who didn't expect that they might have to sell their home or cash in a bank account in order to pay the monthly bills. This is a perfect example of why you must be aware of the maintenance laws in your state before agreeing upon a division of property.

If your current skills don't allow you to support yourself, even working full-time, you may be a candidate for "rehabilitative maintenance." This type of maintenance is paid only for a short time, while you are going to school or getting the training necessary to improve your earning potential. If you find yourself in this position, think strongly about the possibility of obtaining additional training or education. Often, women are not receptive to this idea, believing that it will be too difficult to go back to school and still maintain a household and care for the children. However, consider this option carefully. If you don't, you may find yourself stuck with the same earning potential for many years to come.

If you make more money than your husband, you may be wondering whether you might have to pay him maintenance. Since the laws are gender-neutral, the answer is that the same standards apply when awarding maintenance, whether it is the husband or the wife asking for support. On a practical level, however, it is not common for men to be awarded maintenance, except in unusual circumstances, such as Joan Lunden's case. Consult with your lawyer about whether your situation presents such a rare case to the court, which would theoretically enable your husband to ask for support, and review the guidelines above to determine his likelihood of qualifying for support.

Retirement benefits. Can you receive a part of your husband's pension?

76 percent of retired women receive no pension benefits;

Women are 70 percent more likely to spend their retirement in poverty than men;

One third of all women sixty-five and older live on less than $10,000 per year;

Women sixty-five and older spend one third of their income on medical care.

As these statistics demonstrate, most women in this country have absolutely no retirement benefits. As a result, older women may wind up living on the edge of poverty in their later years. A primary reason is that they are more likely to have stepped out of the work force to raise a family or to have worked part-time. In addition, women often work at jobs that don't typically provide retirement benefits, even after holding the same job for many years.

The good news is that if you are married, you are entitled to a portion of any retirement benefits your husband accrued during the marriage, just as he is entitled to a portion of yours. Retirement benefits are considered an asset of the marriage. Consequently, the court may award you an equal share of your spouse's benefits that accrued during the marriage, or more or less, depending upon the state in which you reside and other facts of your case. Typically, a court will start with the presumption that the benefit which accrued during the marriage should be divided fifty-fifty. A court will then consider any extenuating circumstances that would result in a different division of the benefit. This is true for all types of retirement benefits, whether pension, profit-sharing, or otherwise. Remember that any benefits which you or your husband accrued prior to becoming married are nonmarital and not subject to division by a court.

Retirement benefits include pension and profit-sharing benefits, such as 401(k) plans, as well as stock-option plans. Fortunately, military pensions are now considered marital property. In 1982, Congress passed legislation that, in effect, overruled a decision of the U.S. Supreme Court. The Supreme Court had held that military pensions were not marital property and could not be divided. However, Congress determined that this ruling was extremely unfair to women and passed the Uniformed Services Former Spouses Protection Act, providing that the divorce courts may consider military pensions marital property and divide that asset as the court deems appropriate.

Since retirement benefits may not be paid out until many years after the divorce is final, the benefit is not as easily divided as a bank account or stocks or bonds. Usually, the court divides retirement benefits by entering an order called a Qualified Domestic Relations Order (QDRO). The QDRO states the percentage of the benefit that the court awarded to you or that you and your spouse agreed upon. The QDRO provides that you will begin receiving your portion of the benefit either at the time your spouse retires or at the earliest time that he could retire, regardless of whether he actually continues working or retires.

The alternative to the QDRO is to determine the present

cash value of your rights in this asset and obtain a present lump-sum settlement. If you have been married for a short number of years and your spouse has not participated in the plan for very long, the value of this benefit might be very small. On the other hand, if this has been a long-term marriage and your spouse has been in the plan for twenty or thirty years, your share of the pension or profit-sharing plan could be in the six figures.

It is extremely important that you accurately determine the present and future value of this asset, since it may be the most valuable asset of the marriage. Your attorney may suggest that you retain an accountant or actuary to assist you in this valuation.

Keeping the house vs. selling the house. Which is right for you?

The decision of whether to keep or sell the home is often the most difficult, both financially and emotionally. As a general rule, it is the wife who spent the greater amount of time maintaining the home and locating and coordinating the furniture and furnishings in the home. Most of my clients say their wish is to stay in the home, if at all possible. When there are children involved, the question of whether to stay or sell becomes even more complex.

The problem for most women is that they don't know whether they will be able to afford to keep the house. Often these women have been out of the work force for some time and don't know if it's possible to earn a salary that would allow them to keep the home. Or their finances are so minimal that they literally don't know if they'll be able to put food on the table and still pay the light bill.

The reality is that for many people keeping the house will prove financially difficult. You must consider not only the basic monthly expenses but also the major expenses, such as repair of the roof or replacement of the furnace. There is also the question of whether you will have the time necessary for the upkeep of the property. Consider the normal daily maintenance along with other tasks such as mowing the grass and shoveling the snow. Since you will probably be working full-time, ask yourself whether you will have enough hours in the day to care for the home. It may be too overwhelming.

Use the income/expense form in Appendix A to project as accurately as possible your monthly income and expenses and decide whether you can afford to keep the house. Once you've made that determination, consider the time you will have at your disposal or your inclination to maintain the property. There is absolutely no sense in spending hundreds or thousands of dollars in attorney's fees fighting for the house if you'll just have to sell it anyway.

You may be required to sell the house. For example, if it is basically the only asset of the marriage and your children are grown, you may have to sell. When there are no minor children who need to have a roof over their heads, judges often rule that the house should be sold so that you can have the funds necessary to live. Additionally, the judge may decide that you wouldn't be capable of maintaining the home yourself. Don't cling to your house like a security blanket if it is not financially in your best interests to stay there.

On the other hand, don't give up the house too quickly. Women who have not handled finances often want to throw in the towel when they first realize all the expenses associated with the home and the work necessary to maintain the property. Yet women often don't consider the whole picture. For example, look at all sources of your income available to offset the expenses. This includes child-support payments, your own salary, and perhaps maintenance. You must also consider the benefit of the tax deductions associated with paying the mortgage and taxes, which will provide a refund to you at the end of the year.

Don't assume that you can sell your house and pocket the profit, because the IRS provides a further incentive to keep your home. If you sell your home at a profit, the IRS requires that you pay capital-gains taxes on the amount of the realized profit. In the long run it may be more cost-effective to keep the house, even though you may initially struggle for a few months. Please ask your lawyer to help you determine whether selling or staying is right for you. Don't act hastily or emotionally but, rather, practically.

If you decide that the property should be sold as part of the divorce settlement, be aware of the hidden issues regarding this sale. For example, who will decide the sales price, you or your husband? What if your husband just wants a quick sale so he can take his money and buy a condo? You certainly don't want him selling the property for peanuts. What if the property has been on the market for a month and your husband wants to reduce the price by $20,000? Can he do that? If you decide to sell the property, you must include specific provisions in the settlement agreement regarding this sale. Don't neglect these practical concerns. I have included a sample provision for sale of the real estate in Appendix D.

If you and your husband have decided to divorce and the situation is an amicable one, you may wish to put your house on the market before the papers are filed. Remember, once the papers are filed they become public record. If your house is listed for sale by your lawyer, the real estate broker will know that the house is being sold because of a divorce. There is an old saying in the real estate business: Look for properties involving death or divorce, because in either case you'll get a great deal.

In all cases, consult with your lawyer prior to placing your house on the market.

My husband left us with a lot of debt and ruined our credit rating. How will I be affected?

When couples think about getting a divorce, they usually focus on the issue of "who gets what." There is another side of the equation that most people simply do not consider. That is: Who gets the debts? In many situations, there are no assets to divide, but there is plenty of debt.

Usually the final divorce documents will state that the husband and the wife will each be responsible for paying some debt. For example, each party may retain the note on their automobile. Perhaps each party will be responsible for the charge cards held in his or her name, or perhaps each will be responsible for paying half of all of the charges.

Even if the final agreement waives your responsibility for

paying certain debts, this does not mean that the creditor can't still require you to pay after the divorce is final. The divorce court has the power to divide the debts between you and your husband, but it cannot force the party to whom you owe the money to accept this arrangement. Consequently, you may end up paying a debt that became your husband's responsibility. A typical example will illustrate how unfair this division of debt may be.

Assume that you and your husband owe Visa $1,000 on a joint credit card. The final settlement agreement provides that each of you should pay half of this debt. However, your husband has refused to pay his share. Surely you can't be liable, right?

Wrong. Visa can legally demand that you pay your husband's share of this debt, in addition to your own. This is because when Visa agreed to give you and your husband a charge card, the agreement stated that you would each be responsible for all the charges that were made on that card. Since Visa was not a party to your divorce case, it is not bound to abide by the divorce agreement reached in your case. You both remain liable to Visa for the entire outstanding amount, plus whatever interest has accrued. However, your husband is legally responsible to pay you what he should have paid pursuant to the divorce agreement.

Women are shocked when they learn that they must pay off debts that should have been taken care of by their husbands. Your credit rating can be sabotaged by a nonpaying husband, even though your own payments are current. If you find yourself in this circumstance, there are certain steps you can take.

Be aware of your rights as a debtor and the rights of your creditors. After you have been contacted by a creditor or collection agency, your first step is to determine the total balance due and the amounts your husband should have paid but didn't. Advise them that their bill is delinquent because of your husband's failure to make his payments according to the divorce documents. Most creditors and collection agencies will inform you that the divorce documents are irrelevant as far as they are concerned and that you remain responsible for the balance due.

Decide whether it is financially possible for you to take your husband back to court. Remember, he remains legally liable (to you) to make the payments ordered by the court. If he fails to do so, you may bring him back to court to enforce the court's earlier order. In the meantime, you must determine when you can begin paying the creditor and how much you can afford to pay. The creditor or collection agency realizes that these situations are very common and generally will be willing to work out a payment plan with you. You should not be embarrassed by your husband's failure to pay.

Once you have reached some agreement with the creditor, contact the credit bureau or reporting agency to determine how your husband's refusal to pay has affected your credit rating. If you received a strike against you because of him, contact the agency to determine whether there is any way to remove the black mark from your record. Some agencies will agree to do so after seeing a copy of your divorce papers and receiving a portion of the balance due on the account.

Before agreeing to any property settlement, do your homework. Thoroughly investigate the value of all of the assets of the marriage to determine what is legally available to be divided. If necessary, take depositions and subpoena documents. Then assess your future needs so you can obtain a settlement that will meet your needs and the needs of your children.

Chapter 7

In Their Best Interests: Child Support, Custody, and Visitation

Divorce is always painful, but when children are involved, the emotional and legal issues that a parent must confront can be devastating. You have endless decisions to make about the children. Who will have custody? Should there be joint custody, and if so, where will the children live? What about visitation rights? Which holidays and summers should the children spend with you and which with their father? What if you have concerns about the children being with their father because of physical or sexual abuse? Can your husband take the children out of state?

These questions are only the tip of the iceberg. You must also consider the financial side of the custody and visitation issues. For example, how much will be paid for child support or educational expenses or medical expenses? Will the children continue to attend private school, and what about college?

Unless you know your rights, your husband will be able to

capitalize on a system that gives him a natural advantage. You will be better able to make the necessary decisions once you understand how the laws affect your rights as a parent and the rights of your children.

Child Custody—What Custody Arrangement Is Best for the Children?

True or false: When custody trials are held, judges usually grant custody of the children to the mother.

Believe it or not, this statement is false. Fathers are granted custody approximately 60 percent of the time in cases in which a trial is held. There are many theories as to why this is true. The most common explanation is that men pursue the custody issue all the way through to trial only when they know they have a very good case. For example, if the mother has a substance-abuse problem or has been previously cited for child neglect.

However, because most cases don't go to trial, this statistic sounds worse than it actually is. Over 90 percent of divorce cases never even go to trial. In those situations the husband and wife are able to reach an agreement and resolve the case privately. When such agreements are reached between the parties, women almost always receive physical custody of the children.

Many years ago, the only question parents had to decide was whether the mother or the father would have custody of the children. These days, the question is not that simple. There are different legal custody arrangements from which to choose. The primary options include sole custody, joint custody, and joint parenting.

Sole custody

This is the form of custody that traditionally was most common. A parent who is granted sole custody has the legal authority to reside with the children and to make all decisions affecting the children, including medical and educational. As a general rule, the sole-custodial parent may change the child's residence anytime she deems appropriate. While the thoughts and opinions of the noncustodial parent may be considered, they are of no legal significance and the custodial parent is not bound by the wishes of the noncustodial parent. This differs markedly from the joint-custody arrangement, which provides that both parents have equal decision-making power regarding the lives of the children. Joint custody will be discussed in detail later in this chapter.

Even in a sole-custody situation, the noncustodial parent generally has the right to have visitation with the children. This would not be the case only when the conduct of the noncustodial parent would place the children in danger and, therefore, restriction or elimination of his visitation rights is appropriate. Visitation by a noncustodial parent in a sole-custody situation usually takes place every other weekend, or at such other time as the parties have agreed on.

Over the last several years, it has become less common for women to receive sole custody. One reason is that men are requesting joint custody in greater numbers. While some fathers are sincere in their desire to actively participate in their children's lives, often the request for joint custody is used as a settlement tactic. Men's rights attorneys often counsel their clients to ask for joint custody, even when it is clear that the mother has always been the children's primary caretaker. Under this strategy the hope is that the woman will accept an unfavorable settlement if the father drops his request for joint custody. Unfortunately, this tactic often works.

There are some situations when sole custody is the only acceptable alternative. If, for example, your husband has a history of violence or drug or alcohol abuse, you should hold firm to your request for sole custody. Perhaps the children are very young and your husband has spent little or no time with them. If so, joint custody should not be allowed. Finally, if you and your husband have serious philosophical or religious disputes as to how the children should be raised, sole custody may be the only alternative, since a judge will not allow joint custody in a situation where the parents are unlikely to agree on decisions involving the well-being of the children.

If you have any concerns about your husband's ability to properly care for your children or to work with you in making decisions regarding the children's welfare, you should demand sole custody.

Joint physical custody

Joint physical custody became a popular option approximately fifteen years ago, when certain experts and courts decided that children should live with each parent about equal amounts of time. However, years of experience in monitoring these types of arrangements have shown judges that this form of custody can be extremely difficult on both the children and the parents and may not be a workable solution to the custody problem.

If you have an amicable relationship with your husband and are thinking of agreeing to joint physical custody, make sure the following factors will be present:

1. The mother and father will live close to one another. You don't want the children to feel they are taking a trip every time they switch from Mom's house to Dad's house.

2. The children will be in the same school.

3. The mother and father can afford this arrangement. Since the children spend equal time at each parent's home, they must have duplicate clothes, toys, and other items at both homes, and both homes must be substantial enough to accommodate the number of people living there on a relatively full-time basis.

In a joint-custody situation, each parent is responsible for making decisions relating to the children while they are with that parent. Under most of these arrangements, there are no payments made for child support. Each parent is liable for whatever costs are incurred relating to the children during the time the children are with that parent. Educational and medical costs may be divided equally, or in some other percentage, depending upon the circumstances of the parties.

In some states, the court may not award you and your spouse joint physical custody even if you agree to it. Many judges have seen the aftermath of their prior decisions in this area and have refused to order these types of arrangements. Consider the ramifications very carefully if you are thinking of entering into a physical custody arrangement. By agreeing to joint physical custody, you are telling the court that you have no reservations about your husband having custody of the children. For example, what happens if you later decide you need to move for job reasons? If your spouse doesn't agree, he can probably prevent you from moving and taking the children farther away from him. Before you agree to joint custody, consider that you might be stuck with this situation forever.

Joint parenting

This custody arrangement is actually a combination of sole custody and joint physical custody. Under a joint parenting arrangement, one parent has primary physical custody of the children and the other parent has reasonable, and usually liberal, rights of visitation. For purposes of visitation, joint custody and sole custody often operate similarly. In both situations, noncustodial parents often have visitation every other weekend, and perhaps one day during the week. However, what distinguishes joint custody from sole custody is that in a joint-custody arrangement, both parents have legal custody, which means that they have equal decision-making powers regarding the children's health, education, and welfare. One parent cannot make any major decision without the agreement of the other parent.

Joint parenting, also known as co-parenting, is the arrangement that many courts prefer and is becoming more common. Judges often view co-parenting as the best method of continuing the involvement of both parents in the lives of their children after a divorce. However, joint parenting cannot work unless the mother and father enjoy a good relationship with one another when it comes to raising the children. If you are considering a joint-parenting agreement, the court will look for the following factors to be present:

1. **Both parents can converse civilly and rationally and are capable of having a good relationship** *as parents.*

2. **Both parties have similar views about raising the children.**

3. **The parents have the best interests of their children in mind and will not use the children as pawns to hurt one another or snoop into the life of the other parent.**

Although co-parenting agreements can work very well, I urge you to be cautious about entering into this arrangement, for the same reasons as in the joint-custody situation. By agreeing to co-parenting, you are telling the court that you and your spouse have similar attitudes about raising the children and will be able to work well with one another in making decisions about their welfare. If you have any serious concerns about the parenting abilities of your spouse or his sincerity in working with you to raise the children, a co-parenting agreement is not your best choice.

Temporary custody vs. permanent custody

A temporary Order of Custody will be entered in your case stating where the children will live until the divorce is final. A permanent order will be entered as part of a final settlement agreement, or court decision if your case goes to trial. Divorce attorneys have a saying about custody orders: What is, shall remain. Since your case could take months or years to resolve, a judge is unlikely to upset the lives of the children by switching the custody arrangement when the divorce becomes final.

Therefore, be cautious about entering into a joint-custody or joint-parenting arrangement even on a temporary basis. Unfortunately, many women agree to temporary custody arrangements that they would never accept on a permanent basis. Often mothers are so guilty about the effects of the divorce on their children that they are lulled into thinking that the father should have an equal role in the children's lives—even if this was never the case during the marriage. Women incorrectly believe that since the arrangement is only temporary, there won't be any problem in obtaining sole custody if the situation doesn't work out.

Accepting a liberal custody agreement that gives your husband significant control could easily backfire on you. Do not accept any temporary agreement that you would not be willing to live with on a permanent basis. More than one father has maneuvered his temporary agreement into a permanent one.

111

He suddenly becomes "father of the year" after the temporary agreement is entered, buying the children everything in sight and taking them wherever they wish to go. Of course, the children are delighted and think that Dad's a great guy, while you believe that he is not acting in the children's best interests, but only to further his bad motives. Your husband figures that asking for sole custody won't be so difficult if he uses the time when the temporary order is in effect to show what a terrific father he is. After all, he'll save a bundle in child-support payments every month or at least get you to drop your settlement demands in exchange for either sole custody to you or perhaps even a joint-custody arrangement.

Chances are very good that a judge will make your temporary arrangement permanent, unless you can show that serious problems prevent the arrangement from working forever. Consider all the ramifications before entering into any temporary agreement; it's likely to last a very long time.

The custody ploy—your husband says he wants custody

Nothing is more terrifying to a woman than the possibility of losing custody of her children. The problem is, men and their attorneys are well aware of this fear and capitalize on it. Take the case of Mark and Barb. After Barb filed for divorce, Mark told her, "I've thought long and hard about this, Barb, and I've decided that I want the kids to live with me. I can provide them with a better life financially, and my job is more flexible than yours, so I can spend more time with them. I'm going to ask for sole custody of the children."

This is a typical conversation that is repeated often by fathers who suddenly decide they want their children to live with them. In my experience, 95 percent of the time these men don't want custody. They want property, money, visitation, revenge, and many other things that have nothing to do with custody. The problem is, it's an effective ploy. Most women will compromise their demands when faced with this threat. Usually, it is an empty threat. Remember, over 90 percent of the time cases are settled before they go to trial. However, as I've said, when a judge must decide, women are not necessarily granted automatic custody.

The fact is, however, that the court is still inclined to grant a woman custody if she has been the primary caregiver and is not guilty of any behavior that could harm the children. Nonetheless, when you are on the receiving end of a custody threat, even the outside chance that your husband might get custody scares you. I see too many women who, rather than take that chance, give up everything and take less than they and their children deserve.

To avoid falling victim to this typical ploy:

1. Determine if your husband is serious. Do you believe your husband really wants custody? Has he been a devoted father who spent every spare minute with the children? Most men look at divorce as the road to freedom— they want to be free from responsibility, both to wife and to children. For almost all men, custody gives them more responsibility than they have ever had before. Test your husband. On one or two weekends give him more visitation than he's requested. The odds are very good that he will never even take the children for visitation as often as he is allowed. If so, his threats of getting custody will become absurd, even to his own lawyer.

2. Consider how the court will view your husband. If your husband is like many, he has devoted his life to his business. He probably spends more time at work than anywhere else. Is he a professional who works fifty, sixty, or seventy hours per week? Does he travel frequently or work on weekends? If so, the court will view him as an absentee parent who is unlikely to alter his work style at this point in his life.

On the other hand, if your husband has been "dad of the year," he might have a good chance at custody. This is especially true when the roles are reversed—the woman works many hours and the man is a househusband, or works at home, or has a job with very flexible hours. If your husband has consistently been active in the lives of the children, take his request for custody seriously.

3. Will you be perceived as a good mother? The question is not whether you are a good mom, but whether the court will perceive you as such. Assuming you are not a substance abuser and have taken good care of your children, it will be difficult for your husband to create a perception that you are an unfit parent and that you should not have custody.

Remember, your husband may be simply trying to coerce you into accepting an unfair settlement, under the guise of demanding custody. He might try to embarrass you by revealing that you had an affair, or smoked dope in college, or spent marital money on a face lift. Unless the incidents are recent and paint you as a bad mother, they won't have an impact on custody. As you already know, your conduct may not even be considered a factor in distributing marital property, depending on the state in which your case is proceeding.

Still, review your behavior for something that he might use against you. If there are incidents that call into question your fitness as a parent, your attorney will assess the seriousness of the charges and the effect it may have on a custody determination.

Visitation Schedules and Special Visitation Problems

When physical custody is given to only one parent, the noncustodial parent is entitled to visitation. A typical schedule provides for overnight visitation every other weekend and perhaps an evening during the week. In addition, the children are to split holidays and spend summer vacation with each parent. A complete visitation schedule will be incorporated into the final divorce documents and have the full effect of a court order. A typical visitation schedule can be found in Appendix E.

In some cases, however, it might not be appropriate for your spouse to have visitation with the children. For example, if your husband has a history of violence, substance abuse, or sexual abuse, it may be necessary to prevent all visitation or require supervised visitation. When visitation is supervised, a third party must be present during all times he is with the children. This person should be acceptable to you and to the court, and could be a friend, relative, or professional person, such as a counselor or therapist. If you believe your husband is not entitled to the typical visitation granted to most parents, you must make your concerns known to the court and prove your allegations. A parent has a constitutional right to be with his children and an attempt to limit that right will not be taken lightly.

Unfortunately, it is the rule rather than the exception that noncustodial parents do not follow the visitation schedule. There are few fathers who see their children according to this court order. One reason for this is that fathers frequently ask for more visitation than they really want, simply to harass the mother during the negotiation of the divorce. I wish I had a nickel for every time I've heard: "My husband was supposed to pick up Johnny last Saturday, and he just never showed up. Not even a telephone call." Or "Chuck was supposed to take Susie to a movie, but he said he had to work. She was looking forward to that movie for weeks, and spent the whole day crying." Some situations are downright cruel. I have heard stories of fathers telling their children they were coming right over to drop off a birthday or Christmas present, and then just never showed up. Worse yet, the father may later tell the child that the mother prevented him from dropping off the gift.

These situations are heartbreaking and, sadly, all too common. There is little that can be done to force a man to live up to his agreement to see his children. Of course, the situation is hard not only on the children but on the mother as well. The solution lies in not agreeing to such substantial visitation in the first place. If your husband has requested even the standard visitation, determine whether he is likely to keep to such a schedule or whether he is simply trying to get under your skin. If, for example, you can show that he works weekends, or has other commitments making it nearly impossible for him to stick to the schedule on a consistent basis, don't agree. Each visitation arrangement should be tailored to the real-life schedules of the parents and the children. Agree to only so much visitation as you believe he will use. Remember, you can always give him greater latitude if he demonstrates an ability to stick to the schedule.

Once a visitation arrangement has been established, it is the responsibility of both parents to abide by the schedule. Regardless of your feelings toward your husband, he is entitled to have visitation with the children. Unless you have reason to believe the children would be harmed during visitation with their father, refusing to abide by the visitation schedule is illegal and could result in a change of custody. Visitation is a right of the children, not the parents.

Some visitation problems, though, are much more serious. Kidnapping of children or sexual or physical abuse may occur during periods of visitation.

Child snatching

Last year more than 360,000 children were victims of parental kidnappings. Each state and the federal government have laws aimed at persons who abduct, retain, or conceal children. Child snatching is an offense which can be pursued in both the civil and criminal courts, and carries a prison term if the abductor is found guilty. Each state provides different sentences for this crime.

Child snatching by a parent can only occur if a parent takes the child in violation of a valid existing court order. If there is no court order stating who has temporary or permanent custody of the children, then a parent cannot be guilty of child snatching. Kidnapping by a parent usually occurs when a parent fails to return a child after the end of his visitation period or when he takes the child from a babysitter or from a school environment.

If your husband has *ever* threatened to kidnap your child, or to not return the child after visitation, you must contact the police immediately and file a report outlining the threats your husband made. If he should ever kidnap the child, this report will prove valuable to both the police and to a court of law. After filing the report, contact your lawyer. She may be able to obtain a court order preventing future visitation or requiring supervised visitation because of his threats.

If your child has been abducted, take the following steps:

1. Call your lawyer. She can assist you in outlining a strategy for learning the whereabouts of your husband and child and inform you of the various civil, criminal, and nonprofit agencies you can contact. Additionally, she may call your husband's lawyer to attempt to learn his whereabouts or whether your husband ever advised his lawyer that he intended to kidnap your child. Be aware that even if such was the case, the communication between your spouse and his attorney might be protected under the attorney-client privilege.

2. Call the local police and the FBI. Note, however, that the FBI will become involved only if child snatching is considered a felony under the laws of your state.

3. Contact the Federal Parent Locator Service in Washington, D.C., which provides a national system for locating parents who kidnap their children.

4. Contact the agencies dealing with parental kidnapping of children. Begin with the National Center for Missing and Exploited Children (1-800-843-5678) and Find the Children (1-310-477-6721).

Physical and sexual abuse

In 1990, there were 1.7 million reports of child abuse and more than 200,000 of the children involved were under the age of four. By all accounts, accusations of physical and sexual abuse against children involved in divorce cases are on the rise. The media attention given to the Woody Allen–Mia Farrow case has resulted in greater numbers of people becoming aware of this increasing problem. Although cases of wrongful allegations do occur, studies have shown that false accusations are rare, especially when made by a child. (See David P. Jones and J. Melbourne McGraw, "Reliable and Fictitious Accounts of Sexual Abuse to Children," *Journal of Interpersonal Violence*, March 1987.)

When charges of abuse are made during a pending divorce, the first thing a court is likely to do is appoint a guardian ad litem. This person, usually a lawyer, represents the interests of the child and brings to the attention of the court matters affecting the child's interests. The guardian ad litem will conduct an independent investigation of the alleged incident and interview all parties involved, including the child. The guardian will then report his findings to the court. This report will be instrumental in the court's determination of whether abuse did occur and whether further contact with the abuser will be allowed.

If you believe your child has been physically or sexually abused by your husband, or while in the physical custody of your husband, follow these steps immediately:

1. Contact a physician to conduct a physical examination of the child.

2. If your child is bruised or shows unusual rashes, markings, or scarring, take photographs. If the child is willing to talk about the experience, consider videotaping or audiotaping your child discussing the incident—with as little prompting from you as possible. Such documentation will prove extremely valuable, in both the civil and the criminal court.

3. Consult with your attorney. Discuss whether you should communicate with the child's father, call the police, or contact the state's attorney's office to pursue criminal action against your husband. Depending upon the facts and circumstances, your lawyer may obtain a court order restricting further visitation by the father until the matter is resolved.

4. Find a psychiatrist or psychologist who specializes in child abuse. This mental-health professional can testify at trial after she has interviewed and evaluated your child.

Financial Support for the Children

Every year more than 11 million children are court-awarded or voluntarily promised (by a parent) $15 billion in support. However, less than one third of that amount is ever received. According to a report of the Federal Office of Child Support Enforcement, within six months after a divorce is final, 80 percent of noncustodial parents are behind in payments and no longer visit their children. For an additional 11 million children, support was never even ordered because of problems such as the inability to locate a parent.

Do these statistics scare you? If you are like most of my clients, you probably don't believe that you could be the next statistic. When I speak with women about child support and financial assistance for the children, I often hear: "Oh, you don't have to worry about that. My husband loves his children and has always been very generous. He would never deprive them of anything." Believe me, don't rely on your husband's past conduct when it comes to his financial contribution to raising your children. Even if he has the best of intentions now, you don't know what the future will bring. Chances are that he will remarry and will have another family to support. Once that happens, it is unlikely he will feel as generous as you (or even he) may think.

The fact is, you have a good chance of becoming one of these statistics. One fourth of all women never receive any child support and another fourth receive only partial payment. Your children have a right to receive child support from their father. It is imperative that you understand how much child support your husband should pay and the steps you must take to secure these payments. In addition, there are payments relating to the health and education of your children that your children are entitled to receive.

Child support

What is child support?

The term "child support" refers to the periodic payment made by the noncustodial parent for the care and maintenance of the children. Child support is intended to partially compensate the custodial parent for the basic expenses associated with having custody of the children, such as for food and shelter. Usually, basic child support is not intended to compensate you for other expenses relating to the children, such as medical or educational. Those are additional expenses and will be covered later.

How much child support should I receive?

Nearly every state has laws that specifically determine how much child support the noncustodial parent should pay. These laws are called child-support guidelines. However, they are more than just a guide; they are a legal formula that the court must use to compute child-support amounts.

There are basically two types of formulas used to calculate the proper amount of support. Some states use a formula that prorates the amount of support based upon incomes of both parents. A prorated formula compares your income with your husband's and then factors in the number of children to determine the correct amount of support. Other states use a guideline formula that bases support upon a percentage of the income of the noncustodial parent.

Let's take a typical situation. Michael and Laura have three children and live in Chicago. Michael's net income per month is $2,000. The guidelines for the state of Illinois are:

One child	20 percent of net income of noncustodial parent
Two children	25 percent of net income of noncustodial parent
Three children	32 percent of net income of noncustodial parent
Four children	40 percent of net income of noncustodial parent
Five children	45 percent of net income of noncustodial parent
Six or more	50 percent of net income of noncustodial parent

As you can see, Michael would be required to pay 32 percent of his net income for child support, which is $640 per month. Using this type of guideline, the court may not consider Laura's income, nor may the court consider the ages of the children.

I am often asked the question: "What happens when my husband doesn't declare all of his income? How can we prove how much money he makes?" Proving that your husband has undeclared income is the most common and the most difficult problem we have when it comes to calculating the correct amount of support. However, there are ways to show that your husband has cash income that should be considered for purposes of the support calculation.

Because we are dealing in cash, which is difficult to trace, your testimony regarding your husband's cash income will be extremely important. You must state specifically the type of work your husband does to earn this income and how much he usually makes in cash. Try to obtain the testimony of other friends, family members, or present or former co-workers of your husband to confirm your testimony. Was the money he made used for any particular purpose? Did it pay for the second car, or to repair the house? If certain expenses were always paid for in cash, as opposed to by credit card or check, this may be further evidence of your spouse's having a cash income. Testimony alone can be sufficient for a judge to find that there is undeclared income. The more specific your information about the source and amount of the income, the more likely it is that the judge will believe your testimony and put an additional amount into the income calculation.

Finally, you might be wondering what happens if your

spouse is currently unemployed. Does that mean you'll never receive child support? Certainly not. If your husband has lost his job, and is seeking employment, the court either will order a minimal amount of support during the period of unemployment or will suspend child-support payments until your spouse obtains a job. In some situations the court may believe that your spouse has deliberately become unemployed to avoid his obligations to pay child support. If so, the court might order him to obtain employment and to pay support as if he were working to the level of his capabilities.

What if I need more child support than the guidelines allow?

A child-support order can always be modified if it is in the best interests of the child. However, guidelines were developed so there would be an efficient, predictable, standard method of calculating child support. The judge can make exceptions to the guideline amounts only when there is strong evidence that the amounts are unjust or inappropriate. Be aware that the judge will not deviate from the guidelines unless you have a very unusual set of circumstances.

To increase the guideline amounts, the judge must find that the children have specific needs that are not being met and that the noncustodial parent has the ability to pay a greater amount. The judge may also consider the income of the custodial parent and any other facts relevant to the issue.

Just as it is difficult to increase the guideline amount, it is also difficult to decrease the amount. Husbands often threaten to go to court to reduce the amount of support they are paying.

As a general rule, this will only be done if your husband's income has decreased and the needs of the children have decreased. As every mother knows, the financial needs of children tend to increase as they grow older. As a result, the threat to reduce child support is often just that—a threat. However, reducing support after the judgment will be discussed in more detail in Chapter 12.

How long will I receive child-support payments?

Each child is entitled to support until one of the following events occurs:

- The child reaches the age of majority—usually eighteen.
- The child becomes emancipated—moves away from home, lives independently, and is self-supporting.
- The child dies.

How can I guarantee that my husband will make his child-support payments?

There is no absolute guarantee that you will receive the proper amount of support payments. However, there are steps you can take to increase your chances of receiving the payments.

1. Order of Withholding. At the time your divorce becomes final, the court will enter a permanent order regarding support. This order will state the amount of child support your husband is to pay, either weekly or monthly, depending upon how often he is paid. If your spouse is employed by someone other than himself, almost every state allows the court to enter an Order of Withholding, also called a wage garnishment.

The Order of Withholding will be sent directly to your spouse's employer so that child support will be deducted directly from your husband's paycheck. The check is then sent to you from the employer, or it may first be sent to the court. I recommend that you have the check sent to the court first, if your state provides that option. If you should ever have to take your spouse back to court for nonsupport, the court will have a complete record of all payments that were made and your husband will find it more difficult to claim that he really made payments when the court has a list of every payment received.

You should always have an Order of Withholding entered, because at least it guarantees that your husband cannot receive his check until you receive yours. There is no reason to rely on your husband's good intentions to make these payments if you don't have to. Unfortunately, in some states, such as New Jersey and Mississippi, an Order of Withholding cannot be entered. Furthermore, Orders of Withholding can't be entered if your spouse is self-employed. You must then rely on him to forward your check periodically in the correct amount.

The Order of Withholding is the best method of securing your support payments. However, if entering such an order is not possible, consider having your husband establish security for his child-support obligation in one of the following ways.

2. Pledge collateral. If your husband has a bank account or profit-sharing plan, he can pledge all or a part of that fund to secure his child-support obligation. If he loses his job or stops paying support, you can withdraw the appropriate amount of support from the fund until he begins paying you on a regular basis. This security is especially important when the husband is self-employed and an Order of Withholding cannot be entered. Talk to your lawyer about making such a security agreement part of your final support order.

3. Life insurance. As an additional form of security, most courts will require your husband to maintain a life insurance policy on his life in an amount not less than $100,000. The children must be named as beneficiaries of the policy until they reach the age of eighteen or graduate college, depending upon the terms of the agreement. Your husband will be required to show you proof of the existence of the policy every year until his support obligations to the children terminate.

Do I have to pay taxes on the child support I receive?

No. Child support is not taxable to the receiving parent and is not deductible to the paying parent. In addition, the IRS presumes the custodial parent is entitled to take the children as tax deductions while they are dependents. However, the parents commonly negotiate this issue as part of the settlement agreement. It is not unusual for parents to take the children as dependents in alternating years, or for one parent to declare one of the children and the other parent to declare the other child.

As a general rule, the parent who has the greater income receives the greatest tax advantage from declaring the children as dependents. Since the husband usually has the larger income, he has the most incentive to obtain this benefit. However, if your income is equal to your husband's, make sure that you at least receive the right to take the children in alternating years. If your income is greater than that of your husband, fight for these benefits. Over the years, this tax benefit may save you thousands of dollars.

My husband agreed that if I don't ask for child support he will waive his rights to see the children. Is this legal?

I never cease to be amazed at how often I am asked this question. The answer is no, it is not legal. The right to receive child support is a right of the child—not of the parent. Furthermore, it is the right of a child to have visitation with a parent—even if the parent isn't paying child support. In the eyes of the law, child support and visitation are unrelated issues. Courts recognize that your children need to see both parents, even if one parent can't, or won't, pay to support those children.

If you don't want your husband to have visitation with the children, speak with your lawyer about whether you have grounds to fight his rights to visitation. However, don't fall for the old trick of not pursuing child support because he doesn't see the children. Regardless of a lack of visitation by the non-custodial parent, your children always have the right to be financially supported.

Medical and educational expenses

As stated earlier, in addition to basic child support, you may be entitled to medical, educational, and other financial payments relating to the children. In some states, the basic child-support payment might include these other payments, while in others, the medical and educational expenses are considered to be additions to basic support.

Medical expenses

By some accounts, less than 30 percent of all children in this country are covered by medical/hospitalization insurance. Often, children lose medical coverage when their parents divorce. Your final settlement agreement must include provisions that state which parent will maintain the children on such a policy and how uninsured medical expenses will be paid.

As a rule, "routine" medical expenses are to be covered by the custodial parent, as part of the child support she is receiving. This includes annual checkups and doctor's visits for colds or the flu. However, any other medical or related expenses are considered "extraordinary" and are not covered by the routine child-support check.

Generally, parents who have medical coverage provided by the employer at no or little cost will maintain the children under the policy until they reach the age of eighteen or complete college. A typical agreement will state that at least once a year the parent maintaining such coverage must provide proof of coverage to the other parent, along with insurance cards for the children.

Any unpaid expenses not covered under the policy must either be divided between the parties or paid solely by one of the parents. Usually the parties divide the expenses in proportion to their incomes or share the expenses equally. A parent who earns a disproportionately greater income than the other will usually become solely responsible for uninsured medical expenses. In either case, each parent's responsibility for payment of medical expenses should be spelled out clearly in the settlement or parenting agreement.

The following expenses are included under the broad term "medical": medical, hospitalization, dental, orthodontic, ophthalmological, psychological, and counseling for specific disorders, such as learning disabilities.

Particularly if you have a child with a medical or related disability, your final divorce documents must include provisions for the continuation of the children's medical coverage and payments for unpaid expenses.

Educational expenses

Like medical costs, educational expenses are often considered an expense that must be paid in addition to basic child support. If so, your divorce documents must state who will pay for grammar school, high school, and college educational costs. If your children are under the age of six, payment must be made for day care or preschool.

Educational expenses are usually divided equally between the parents or pro rata, based upon the incomes of the parties. If the children are quite young, the documents often provide that the issue of education will be "reserved" to a later time. This means that the parties have agreed to wait until the children are older to decide these issues, since they are years away from attending a particular school or college. In addition, the parties will be in a better position to determine who can pay for educational expenses years later, and the child will have had an opportunity to establish his interests and abilities.

Be careful, though. What happens if ten years from now your income exceeds your husband's? If a court has reserved the issue or you have divided costs pro rata, you may end up paying more than 50 percent of your child's educational costs. Consider this issue carefully before agreeing to "reserve" the issue or to divide the cost either equally or pro rata. Estimate as best as possible your future income and your husband's future income to arrive at an agreement that would be fair to you and your children.

Chapter 8

To Trial or
Not to Trial

As you know by now, over 90 percent of all divorce cases never go to trial. In some areas the chances of your going to trial are less than 1 in 1,000. Usually the parties resolve their differences by entering into a property settlement agreement and a parenting agreement. This agreement may be reached a month after filing for divorce or years later, on the eve of trial. You've probably heard the saying that cases often settle "on the courthouse steps."

At some point you will have to decide whether to settle your case or go to trial. For some people, the decision is easy. If there are few assets, large debts, and no disputes about custody, chances are the case will settle. On the other hand, it may be so obvious that an agreement cannot be reached that it is a foregone conclusion that a trial must take place.

However, in most situations the decision about whether to settle or to go to trial is more complicated. What if a reasonably good proposal has been offered but you wonder if you'd get more by fighting? Or what if you simply want to wait until the last moment, thinking that your spouse won't want to go to trial and will eventually give in to your demands? Going to trial is a last resort and the decision to try a case should not be made without seriously considering all the ramifications.

Women often suffer from the "I want my day in court" syndrome. They have been through miserable marriages that lasted many years and now want to tell their story to the judge. Women want their husbands to admit to all the rotten things they did during the marriage and want their husbands to pay for what they did. Unfortunately or not, those days are gone. Conduct of the spouses is completely irrelevant in many cases. Some critics charge that we should bring back the old days and require men to account, financially and otherwise, for conduct such as cheating, battering, drinking, and gambling. Until then, judges who have hundreds of cases to deal with are not going to allow you to take up their time by telling them the story of your life.

If you decide to go to trial, make sure it is for the right reasons. Consider the following in determining whether to resolve your case by entering into a settlement agreement or taking the case to trial.

Alternatives to Trial

A major factor that often determines how a case will proceed is attorney's fees. Where there is substantial wealth, attorney's fees are, of course, not a major concern. The parties can settle or try as they deem appropriate, without regard for fees. On the other hand, if there are no assets available to pay for attorney's fees, it will not be possible to go to trial, unless you intend to represent yourself.

What is more common, however, is a situation where going to trial is not financially in the best interests of either you or your husband. The case of Howard and Janet is typical. They separated one year ago, after being married for twenty years. Howard moved into an apartment and contributes to Janet's household bills. Janet remains in the home with their two children, Neal and Nancy. Neal is nineteen years old and attends a local college; Nancy is in high school. Howard and Janet both work full-time, and Howard makes about $20,000 per year more than Janet. The assets consist of their house, which has equity of $100,000, two automobiles, and a couple of small bank accounts. Howard wants to sell the house and divide the proceeds fifty-fifty. Janet wants to stay in the house until Nancy graduates from high school, and then split the profits 65 percent to her and 35 percent to Howard. So far, Howard and Janet have not been able to reach an agreement. Should Janet go to trial?

There are two answers to that question—the legal and the practical. The legal answer is that Janet should go to trial. While there are no guarantees, it is likely that she would receive a greater percentage of the house due to the disparity of income between her and Howard. Since her younger child is still in school, chances are fairly good that she would be able to stay in the house until Nancy completes high school. Does this mean that Janet should inform her attorney to start preparing for trial?

In this situation, probably not. The practical side of this

issue is that if Janet were to go to trial, her attorney's fees are likely to be a minimum of $10,000, and perhaps more. Even if the judge did award her 65 percent of the house, after the costs of attorney's fees she would be receiving only $5,000 more than what Howard was willing to give her. Additionally, she has only a fifty-fifty chance of staying in the house. Further, if the trial lasts longer than expected, the attorney's fees will be greater and Janet could end up with less than what Howard had offered in the first place.

Of course, the problem is that this just doesn't seem fair. Under the law, Janet may be entitled to about 65 percent of the value of the house and may be allowed to stay in the house until Nancy graduates. Howard has figured out what most people come to learn—that is, even if Janet goes to trial, she might receive approximately the same amount that Howard offered (and so might just as well have saved herself and the children the time and trouble of a trial). Or, after paying attorney's fees, she might receive less. What would you do if you were Janet?

Some people in Janet's position decide to go to trial, figuring that even if they end up with the same amount of money that Howard offered, at least they have the satisfaction of not giving in. Other people will settle, thinking that they'd rather keep the money in their own pockets than give it to the lawyers. Both positions have merit. If I were counseling Janet, I would discuss both of those options and offer her some other alternatives.

Alternative 1: Tell Howard
you're going to trial

One of the best alternatives for Janet might be to tell How-ard that she intends to go to trial unless he offers her more than 50 percent of the house. This doesn't mean, however, that Janet will ultimately go to trial. It may simply be in her best interests to delay the case. In some cities it might be a very long time before Janet's case goes to trial. Particularly in a large metropolitan area, such as New York, Los Angeles, or Chicago, a year or more might pass before the trial begins, because of the extensive backlog of cases. If that is true where you live, you can use the courthouse delay to your own advantage.

Since Howard is still contributing to the household bills, and Janet wants to stay in the house until Nancy graduates, it might be best for Janet to delay the case as long as possible. By the time her case is ready for trial, she might decide to settle fifty-fifty "on the courthouse steps." In most cases, a party's earlier offer will still be available on the day of trial. In the meantime, Janet and the children can continue to live in the house and Howard must continue to contribute to paying the monthly bills.

But there are drawbacks to this strategy that you should be aware of. As you get closer to the actual trial date, both your lawyer and your husband's lawyer must begin preparing the case as if there will be a trial. Obviously, they must be ready in the event you don't intend to settle. Once your lawyer begins preparing for trial, your attorney's fees begin to mount. Conse-quently, you can bluff for only so long. At the point when your attorney begins preparing, you must decide which path you intend to pursue: settlement or trial. If your real intent is to eventually settle, you don't want to be paying a lawyer to get ready for a trial that won't take place.

There is another risk in following this plan, although it is a minor one. Your husband may call your bluff by withdrawing his fifty-fifty offer and forcing you to go to trial. Technically, offers are "open" only as long as the party making the offer decides to make it available. I would consider this a minimal risk. Offers usually remain open until the time of trial, since most people are interested in avoiding a trial, if at all possible.

Still another alternative is available to Janet.

Alternative 2: Pretrial

A pretrial with the judge can be considered a poor man's trial. It is a way of finding out how the judge would rule in your case, without going through an actual trial.

A pretrial is a conference that takes place in the judge's chambers between the judge, the attorneys, and, sometimes, the parties. The discussion is "off the record," meaning there is no court reporter taking down what is said. Before the pretrial each attorney must prepare and present the judge with a pre-trial memorandum which summarizes each side's view of the case and their position regarding how the case should be set-tled. After the judge reviews the memorandums, he meets with the attorneys in his chambers to discuss the case and to make his recommendation. Some judges then meet with the parties, while others have the attorneys advise the parties of the judge's recommendation.

If the judge's recommendation is approximately what

you've asked for, your husband should be convinced that you will prevail if you do go to trial. In fact, it is possible that the judge could recommend that you receive more than you've asked for, which would really be powerful ammunition to convince him to settle on your terms.

Your major pretrial risk is that a judge may recommend that you accept your husband's settlement offer. Though the judge's recommendation isn't binding, it's difficult to ignore. In many cases, the pretrial judge will become your trial judge. If so, it's doubtful that a full-blown trial will change his mind about your case, and he probably won't be happy if you turn down his settlement recommendation and force him to spend his valuable time on a case that he thinks should have settled.

Janet has yet another alternative.

Alternative 3: Make a counteroffer

Janet proposed a 65–35 split, providing she keep the house for two years. Howard offered an equal split of the profits and wants the house sold now. Rather than hastily deciding to go to trial, perhaps it's time for Janet to consider making a counteroffer.

Before doing so, Janet must consider both practical and financial issues. For example, she must decide how important it is to stay in the house until Nancy graduates. Janet might think Nancy wants to stay until she graduates, while Nancy might be happy to leave the house and the memories it holds. Janet must also decide whether it is more cost-efficient for the case to continue, so that Howard must contribute to paying the bills, or whether Janet would simply prefer to get the whole case over with and move on with her life.

The divorce process tends to make even the most reasonable men and women unreasonably obstinate. I've found, however, that women find it easier to move from their original positions whereas men take a macho, no-compromise stance. Use this ability to come up with creative suggestions about how to reach a settlement. This doesn't mean that Janet gives Howard what he wants, but it does mean that Janet will take the initiative and be the one who finds the middle ground. Invariably, the party that comes up with the compromise has greater control than the person who reluctantly agrees to go along.

For example, Janet might suggest to Howard, without prodding from him, that he take more of the items from the house, such as the furniture and furnishings, than he requested. Men often feel that they are being shortchanged because they receive fewer of the items accumulated during the marriage. By offering your husband an additional television or that extra couch and chairs, you might very well get a quicker and better settlement, by receiving an additional percentage of his pension or some other asset or concession, which more than compensates you for the items that you gave to your husband.

Janet has one last alternative available.

Alternative 4: A four-way settlement conference

Sometimes the only way to resolve a case is to put all the parties in the same room at the same time and decide no one leaves until the case is settled. Attorneys commonly refer to these meetings as "four ways," at which the husband, the wife, and each of their lawyers are present.

A settlement conference can be particularly helpful when there have been miscommunication problems. For example, the wife will tell her attorney about a problem she is having with her husband, and by the time the husband hears about this problem from his lawyer, the husband swears that the wife made up half of the story. Something always seems to get lost in the translation.

Problems involving miscommunication are very common. Men's egos are easily threatened by the divorce process, and they can blow up a secondhand statement, misinterpreting what was meant and creating a roadblock to settlement where there should be none.

If you are experiencing this problem, a settlement conference is the best alternative for you. It gives everyone an opportunity to speak their mind and discuss their individual problems and concerns. Sometimes men (and women) simply want a forum where there is a captive audience and have an opportunity to "hold court." Once he's had an opportunity to get certain things off his chest, settlement often occurs. With all the participants in the same room at the same place and time, everyone has an opportunity to speak their mind and make their positions understood. Miscommunication problems are eliminated and everyone can get down to the business at hand of resolving the situation.

Attorneys tend to suggest settlement conferences in almost all cases. This is because the parties tend to be more reasonable while they are together, as opposed to talking at each other through their lawyers. On the other hand, there are some people who literally cannot be in the same room with their spouse. Some men try to intimidate their wives during these conferences, perhaps because they have done so throughout their marriages. Often women tell me that if they attend, they will simply agree to all of their husband's demands just to get the meeting over with. If this is true for you, make clear to your lawyer that you would not be comfortable attending a settlement conference at which your husband is present. As an option, you might offer to be available by telephone and attempt to reach an agreement while your lawyer represents you at the meeting.

Settlement vs. Trial: The Pros and Cons

Question: When have you reached a good settlement?

Answer: When neither side is happy.

Every lawyer is familiar with this saying about settlements. One divorce court judge puts it this way: "A good settlement is when one party pays more than he wanted and the other party takes less than she wanted."

Chances are very good that you will not end up with a settlement that gives you everything you asked for. The same is true for your husband. The objective is to reach a settlement that is acceptable to you—not one that you will necessarily be happy with. The alternative, of course, is going to trial. The question is whether a trial is the best option for you.

A trial can be difficult, expensive, and time-consuming. It can be emotionally draining on you and your children, particularly if custody is an issue and the children will have to testify. Trials are also open to the public, so you must be prepared to have your case heard before a group of strangers, or neighbors, friends, or family, if they decide to attend. There are right reasons and wrong reasons for going to trial.

Consider going to trial if

1. You have nothing to lose. If the settlement proposal made by your husband is very low compared with what the court is likely to award you, you are a good candidate for trial.

2. You can afford the attorney's fees required for going to trial.

3. There are issues of custody and visitation that cannot be resolved through settlement or mediation.

4. You are emotionally prepared to go through a trial.

5. You have reasonable expectations of what the court will award.

6. You are doing it for the right reasons, not out of hostility or revenge.

Don't go through a trial if

1. You are disputing minor points or relatively small amounts of money (compared with the cost of trial). Don't refuse to

settle because of housewares, furniture, or other items that can easily be replaced.

2. You are asking for the impossible. If your settlement demands are completely unreasonable, you are not likely to get much sympathy from a judge at trial.

3. You are asking for the ridiculous. Even if your husband was a miserable jerk to you, the judge is not likely to draw and quarter him just to make you happy.

4. You can't afford the necessary attorney's fees. Don't squander your marital assets on attorney's fees if it isn't likely to pay off for you in the end.

5. You are arguing over "the principle of the matter." Never go to trial unless it makes good financial and legal sense.

6. You are doing it for reasons of revenge or hostility.

Custody Trials

Anyone who has been involved in a custody trial knows that there truly are no winners. A custody battle is traumatic for all those involved—parents, children, and even judges, lawyers, and experts. Yet, sadly, some cases cannot be resolved without going through the nightmare of trying to split the baby in two.

In some states, parents are not entitled to pursue a custody trial unless they first go through the process known as mediation. Mediation is an alternative form of dispute resolution. A third party, called a mediator, helps parents to reach an agreement regarding their children that is acceptable to both. (Mediation will be discussed at greater length in Chapter 14.) Thankfully, mediation resolves a number of cases that would otherwise have been destined for World War III in the courtroom. Unfortunately, there are still too many cases that require a judge to decide where the children will live and with whom.

If mediation is not mandatory in your state but you wish to resolve custody without going to trial, talk with your lawyer about private mediation. You owe it to yourself and your children to avoid the ordeal of a custody trial if at all possible.

Notwithstanding all your efforts, it may be impossible to avoid a trial on the issue of custody. If so, the court will determine which parent provides the most appropriate environment for the children and, in general, what custody arrangement would be in the children's best interests. Of course, the court considers numerous factors before making such a profound decision. Some of the most important factors are:

the parent's wishes

the child's wishes

**where and with whom the child has been living
(which parent had temporary custody)**

**the possibility of joint custody
(could the parents cooperate?)**

age and sex of child and parents

financial circumstances of each parent

alleged misconduct of either parent

(substance abuse, physical/sexual abuse, child neglect or abandonment)

In addition to these factors, the court may consider any other information it deems relevant. For example, a judge may allow evidence of the father's failure to pay child support or his cohabitation with a member of the same, or opposite, sex. The court will look to how much time each parent would be able to spend with the children if granted custody, and whether granting custody to a parent would require the children to move or change schools.

All custody cases involve the "battle of the experts." By the time of trial, both parents have retained psychologists, psychiatrists, or other professionals to testify that each would make a better custodial parent. Judges are entitled to consider the experience and expertise of the professional in weighing the importance of their testimony. Your expert will be an extremely important part of your case—and may tip the scales in your favor or against you. Therefore, before retaining your experts, review their credentials very carefully. Look for someone

with a particular expertise in child-custody matters,

who has testified before, and

who can state clearly that you would be the better custodial parent for the child.

Your lawyer will assist you in locating experienced and qualified experts to testify in your case.

One myth regarding custody cases that still exists has to do with what lawyers call the "tender-years doctrine." The law used to presume that mothers were the proper custodial parent when a child was of "tender years," which usually meant under the age of six. As a result, many women still assume that if a child is extremely young, custody will automatically be granted to the mother.

However, in the 1970s and 1980s, courts struck down the tender-years doctrine, stating that men and women should be on an equal footing when it comes to custody of their children. Notwithstanding this change, note that the above list of factors includes a consideration for the age and sex of the children and the parents. While the law no longer presumes that the mother is the better parent, clearly the courts still emphasize these factors and, in the opinion of some experts, still prefer to award custody to women, especially when children are young—although custody awards are no longer automatic by any means.

Another myth involving custody determinations is that courts give custody to one parent or the other on the basis of one individual factor or event. However, courts rarely single out one reason or event that caused them to grant custody to one parent or the other. Don't fall victim to your husband's threats that he'll tell the judge all about your little "secret" and end up winning custody. Just because you smoked a joint twenty years ago doesn't mean that the court will give your husband custody. The judge will consider all the facts and circumstances when deciding which parent should receive custody, or whether joint custody would be appropriate. However, prior to reaching that point, make every effort to resolve the situation without subjecting the children to an experience they'll never forget and, perhaps, never overcome.

Before deciding whether to settle your case or to go to trial, consider the practical and legal effects and explore all the available settlement options. While you shouldn't be bullied into settling because of your husband's threats to go to trial, don't have a judge decide your fate unless you're willing to live with the result.

Chapter 9

Prenuptial Agreements— Do They Hold Up? Sign One and You Might Find Out

Prenuptial agreements are not just for movie stars anymore. People like you and me are entering into prenuptial agreements at an ever-increasing pace. By some estimates, the use of prenuptial agreements tripled between 1978 and 1988. Demographics show why these contracts are on the rise.

Studies show that men and women are waiting to marry until their mid- to late twenties; many professionals wait until their thirties. By the time they decide to marry, they have accumulated enough assets to be thinking about preserving their rights to them. Often they have come from divorced homes and know that divorce is something that can happen to them. In addition, the number of second and third marriages has been on the rise for the last twenty years. When marrying again, spouses are primarily concerned about providing for the children from their previous marriage.

The most common question attorneys receive about prenuptial agreements is: "Do they really work?" People tend to assume that these agreements are easily broken by sharp lawyers, possibly because the media tends to focus on cases in which prenuptial agreements are being contested. Take the case of Sylvester Stallone and Brigitte Nielsen, or Joan Collins and her husband. In both situations the media played up the fact that Sylvester and Joan had gone through the trouble and expense of having a prenuptial agreement signed, and yet here they were in court, still having to battle it out with their spouses. Yet most people never realize that prenuptial agreements do work—when the rules have been followed. In fact, both Sylvester and Joan were successful in having their prenuptial agreements upheld.

While women can use prenuptial agreements to protect their assets in the same manner as men do, the odds are that you've signed one at your husband's request (or insistence). If so, you need to know if the agreement is fair, valid, and enforceable. First, though, we need to clear up some common misconceptions about the purpose of a prenuptial agreement.

What rights are waived in a prenuptial agreement?

A prenuptial agreement limits your legal rights in the event the marriage ends by divorce or death. In many states the law provides that when a husband dies, his wife is automatically entitled to a certain portion of his assets—no matter what his will says. Because you are his "surviving spouse" you could receive anywhere from one third to 100 percent of his estate.

However, if you sign a prenuptial agreement waiving your rights, the agreement will override the law.

As you know, spouses are entitled to a division of marital property in the event of divorce, which may be fifty-fifty or some other percentage. Rather than leaving such a division to the court, a husband will ask his wife to sign a prenuptial agreement which restricts her to a certain percentage or dollar value of the marital property. Some prenuptial contracts limit the rights of a spouse only in the case of death or only in the case of divorce. Most, however, cover both circumstances.

A postnuptial agreement is exactly the same as a prenuptial agreement, except that it is entered into after the marriage has taken place. The requirements for finding such agreements valid are the same for both pre- and postnuptials. There is no time limitation as to when a postnuptial can be signed. I know of one case where the parties entered into a postnuptial agreement after twenty-five years of marriage.

Are prenuptial agreements enforceable?

Yes, these agreements are enforceable—but only when all of the rules are followed. Although the law differs from state to state, a prenuptial agreement will be upheld by a court

if it is fair,

if it was entered into voluntarily, and

if it was entered into in good faith.

151

But what do those terms mean? For example, you and I might think that Joan Collins was "fair" (or more than fair) when she agreed to give her young husband 20 percent of her income for each year they were married. But would a court think that's fair? Why not 10 percent or 30 or 40 percent? As you can see, what makes an agreement "fair" can be difficult to determine, even for a judge. Similarly, it may be difficult to decide whether the agreement was entered into "voluntarily," without duress or coercion, and whether it was entered into in "good faith."

There are three basic questions the court will ask to determine whether the contract was entered into freely, fairly, and in good faith. They are:

1. When was the agreement entered into?

The closer you are to the date of the marriage, the greater the chance that the court will hold that the agreement was not entered into voluntarily and should not be upheld.

For example, the morning of your wedding, Bob suddenly presents you with a prenuptial agreement. He says that his accountant "forced" him to have these papers drawn up, to protect his business in the event of a divorce. You and Bob have never even discussed a prenuptial agreement, so this comes as quite a shock. Bob says that he waited until the last minute because he never found a good time to bring up the issue. He assures you that this is not as big a deal as you are making it, that he loves you dearly, and that he'll always "take care of you" if anything should happen. However, Bob says he won't go ahead with the wedding unless you sign. The ceremony is only hours away. What should you do?

If you were to call a lawyer right now and ask for advice, she would probably tell you to go ahead and sign the agreement—if you still wanted to marry Bob. That is because in many states there is no way such an agreement would be upheld. Your testimony will prove to the judge that Bob's conduct, only hours before the ceremony, was threatening and coercive and would cause the court to invalidate the agreement.

You may wonder when a prenuptial agreement should be signed. While there is no definite schedule, a month or more before the wedding would be considered reasonable in most states.

2. Was there full disclosure before the agreement was signed?

Did you know how wealthy your husband was before signing the contract? Was a listing of his assets and debts attached to the agreement? If not, it is unlikely that a judge will find the agreement valid, regardless of when it was executed.

As a general rule, *both* spouses must reveal all of their assets and debts—even the "nonmonied" or "poor" spouse. This is because the agreement provides for payments to the nonmonied spouse in the event of death or divorce. If that spouse has greater assets than she disclosed, her husband might not have provided as much to her in the agreement.

The disclosure must be complete, and include all income, expenses, assets, and debts, and also provide correct valuations for the assets. The problem is, husbands use certain tricks to avoid making true and accurate disclosures. If you are considering entering into a prenuptial agreement, you can avoid falling victim to these tricks by asking the following questions:

How do his current finances compare with last year's?

If he only gave you a disclosure for this year, you would not know whether his income or assets were more or less than average. Take the following example: Your husband says that this year he earned $250,000. On the basis of that figure, you sign a prenuptial agreement stating that in the event of divorce you will receive 25 percent of the marital property. You later learn that he usually makes double or triple that amount and that "coincidentally" he was having a bad year when the disclosure was made.

Request a disclosure for the last three years to make sure you have the complete financial picture. Also, ask for backup documentation to substantiate the figures, such as tax returns, trust agreements, and brokerage statements.

Did he sell any property just before signing the agreement?

If your husband didn't want to disclose certain assets, he could simply sell the assets prior to making the disclosure. That way, he would be technically correct in stating that he only "owned" certain assets as of the date of the disclosure. Prevent this from happening by requesting a listing of all assets which have been sold or transferred within the three-year period prior to making the disclosure.

Does he have interests in property on which his name does not appear?

Your husband might have assets in some type of trust or held in someone else's name for his benefit. If so, the disclosure might not include such property. Make sure you ask for an inventory of all assets in which he has an interest, present or future, regardless of whose name the property is titled in. Go back at least three years.

If you follow these suggestions, even the most clever husband will have to accurately disclose his true net worth.

3. Were you represented by a lawyer?

This is probably the most important factor a judge will look for in determining whether the requirements exist to uphold the agreement.

- If you were not represented by an attorney, chances are very good that the contract will not be upheld. Rights that you acquire through marriage are so basic that the law considers it essential that a lawyer advise you of the ramifications of waiving any of these rights.

- If you were represented, was the lawyer chosen by your husband? Were his fees paid by your husband? If so, the court is not going to be much happier than if you had no lawyer at all. The judge wants to see that you and your husband were independently represented. Did your lawyer fully and openly explain every part of the agreement before it was signed? A lawyer hired and paid for by your husband might be willing to look the other way when difficult issues arise, as compared with a lawyer you hired.

- Did your lawyer give you a copy of the agreement before it was signed for your review? Did you receive one after it was signed? If not, a court is likely to be suspicious of whether you were represented by competent, independent counsel primarily concerned with your best interests, and not your husband's.

I signed a prenuptial agreement and don't think it's fair. What should I do?

Many women who sign a pre- or postnuptial agreement never even consider contesting the agreement when the marriage ends. They assume that since it was prepared by a lawyer and they signed it, the document must be valid. As we have seen, that is far from the case. However, once you've signed such an agreement, you have given your spouse a good deal of legal ammunition. It's even worse if you signed a second agreement which revised the first. While it might be possible to contest one agreement, two are very tough to fight against. If you've signed one agreement already, whatever you do, don't sign a second one. If you've signed one agreement and now believe the terms are unfair, don't just give in to your husband. Follow these steps:

- **Take the agreement to a lawyer and get an opinion about its validity.** As you've already seen, there are a number of ways to attack a prenuptial agreement. Chances are good that all the rules weren't followed before the contract was signed. If so, your odds of winning on that basis alone might be very good.

- **Call his bluff, even if your chances aren't great.** It will cost your husband a good deal of money in legal fees to prove that the agreement is valid. Use that as a bargaining tool to obtain a settlement which is more favorable than the terms of the agreement. Be aware that you might not be able to get much—maybe a small sum of money or maintenance for six months or a year. Don't expect a windfall, but it's probably worth your effort to bluff and go for it.

- **If the agreement seems to shortchange the children, don't hesitate to fight.** Even if all of the rules were followed, a court will not uphold provisions that are unfair to the children. Women are often unaware that the rights of a child can *never* be lost because of a prenuptial agreement. Don't fail to fight for your children's rights because of this piece of paper. If the document states that child support or medical or educational expenses will be eliminated, or will be less than the law requires, don't believe it. A court won't uphold provisions that hurt the children.

I've heard that prenuptial agreements don't apply to retirement benefits. Does that mean I can get a share of my husband's pension even though I signed a prenup?

Most prenuptial agreements contain waivers of the wife's rights to the husband's retirement plans. However, recent court cases have held that such waivers might not be valid. If so, you may be entitled to a portion of your husband's pension or profit-sharing plan, even if the rest of the prenuptial agreement is found to be valid.

Because the law in this area is in a state of flux, it is imperative that you consult with an attorney if your prenuptial agreement contains provisions waiving rights to retirement benefits.

Are prenuptial agreements fair? Should I sign one?

Everyone has their own opinion on this subject. Divorce lawyers themselves often disagree about whether prenups are a good idea. Some say women almost always get the short end of the stick. Since men have always been more affluent in our society, prenups generally tend to protect men's assets, to the detriment of women. Others say such agreements are needed to save a prosperous, hardworking spouse from "gold diggers" (both male and female) and to protect children from previous marriages. Some people actually accuse lawyers of encouraging divorce by recommending prenuptial agreements. They say that by focusing on the dissolution of the marriage, the couple starts off on the wrong foot and doesn't psychologically make the long-term commitment needed for a marriage to last. On the other hand, considering whether to sign a prenup has the effect of forcing a couple to discuss how they'll handle their finances after they're married.

Like it or not, prenups have become a fact of life, and if you decide to remarry, you shouldn't be surprised if a prenup is part of the package. Whether or not his reasons for requesting that you sign it are valid, you should know exactly what you're getting yourself into and how it may be used against you and your children.

Chapter 10

Living Together,
Living Apart—
Strategies for Cohabitation
in the 1990s

Living in sin, playing house, "just living together" —whatever you call it, more and more couples are cohabiting. According to the Census Bureau, in the last ten years the number of unmarried households has grown 80 percent. It is estimated that one out of two Americans lives with a partner before marrying for the first time and almost half of all women between the ages of twenty-five and thirty-four have lived with a partner.

The common perception of people living together is that they have never been married and have no children. However, cohabitation is actually more common among the separated and divorced than among the never-married. Forty percent of couples living together have children, most of whom are from previous marriages.

You would think that living together before marriage would make divorce less likely. Unfortunately, living together is no guarantee of staying together. Statistics show that couples who cohabit before marriage are 50 percent more likely to break up. The experts suggest that one reason for this increased divorce rate is that those who live together are less conservative and traditional, making divorce a more acceptable solution when the marriage doesn't work out. Others suggest that when a problem arises between a couple living together, the solution is often to get married, rather than to separate or resolve the issue fully. After marriage, the problem remains, but the couple may blame the marriage itself for "just not working" rather than focusing on the problem.

Before moving in with your partner, you probably thought about all the money you'd save on rent payments. Chances are that you never thought about the legal ramifications of entering into such a relationship. Like many women, you didn't know the rights and obligations that the law imposes on those who live together. For example, did you ever consider what would happen if you were to break up with your partner? If both of your names are on the lease, who keeps the apartment and pays the rent? Who gets to keep the television and furniture that you bought together?

If children are involved, the issues become even more complex. Do you know whether your partner could wage a custody fight for the children born during the relationship? On the other hand, what if he decides to walk away and never pay child support?

Finally, there is the matter of "palimony," which we've all

heard about. Do you really know what it is and whether you'd qualify?

In most cases, living together still favors the man rather than the woman. Kathy's case is typical. She and Steve moved in together five years ago. Steve makes about twice what Kathy does, but they agreed to split all bills equally. A couple of years ago they bought a house, but put the house in Steve's name because he contributed more to the down payment. When Steve decided to break up with Kathy, she was forced to move out since the house was in his name. He refused to reimburse her for the money she had paid toward the mortgage and only allowed her to take the furniture that she had before they were together. Kathy was left with no money and nowhere to live. At the end of the relationship she had less than what she started with.

Women who live with their partners are vulnerable because they're not protected by rights of marriage. The longer a woman lives with her partner, the more she stands to lose. If he should leave her, she will have none of the rights a spouse is entitled to. Even though she lived with the man for years, as if they were married, and contributed to the relationship by taking care of the household and the children, the only thing that matters is whether they were married. Although a wife may be entitled to medical benefits, spousal maintenance, and a property distribution, this woman has no such rights and is left with nothing.

As you can see, living together may result in more than just saving a rental payment each month. Couples who live together and then terminate their relationship face many of the same issues that divorcing couples must deal with. However, since you were never legally married, you may end up with none of the legal rights but many legal responsibilities for which you were not prepared. Before deciding to move in with your partner, be aware of the serious legal ramifications that can affect you and your children.

Common-Law Marriage

True or false: In most states, if you have lived with your partner for at least seven years, you have a common-law marriage.

The answer is false. Most states do not recognize any form of common-law marriage. This means that you could live with your partner forever and still never be entitled to any of the legal rights guaranteed to spouses. Although living together is quite common, the law has been slow to legitimize this type of relationship. Some experts believe that the primary reason is that only traditional marriages should be encouraged and, therefore, validated by the law.

The other major misconception about living together is that you can end such a relationship by just walking away, without the hassle of going through a divorce. Not so. If you do live in one of the few states that recognize common-law marriages and you can prove that such a marriage exists, a divorce is required to terminate the relationship. Once a common-law marriage is established, it becomes the legal equivalent of a traditional marriage, with the same rights and obligations imposed upon spouses.

When a woman decides to live with her partner rather than marry, she is giving up substantial legal rights of which she is not even aware. When the relationship ends, she may be financially left with nothing—and the law can't help her. The story of Dolores and Frank illustrates the problems a woman encounters when she cohabits with her partner.

Frank and Dolores met in 1950, when they were eighteen years old. They were madly in love, but both of their parents objected to their marrying. As a result, Frank and Dolores left their small town and went to Chicago to marry. They thought a big city would provide many opportunities and a chance to make a new life for themselves without the interference of their families. Dolores and Frank both worked full-time until they began having a family. When Dolores had their third child, she became a full-time mother and homemaker.

Years later, after all their children were grown and out of the house, Frank told Dolores that he had met someone else and intended to spend the rest of his life with her. Frank moved out and Dolores didn't know where to turn. Dolores knew that after all these years their secret would become very public. As you have probably guessed by now, Frank and Dolores never did get married. When Frank left, they had been together almost twenty-five years.

Unfortunately for Dolores, the state of Illinois, like many states, does not recognize common-law marriage. Dolores was financially and emotionally devastated. She had no rights under either state or federal law. Dolores was not entitled to a portion of Frank's pension or profit-sharing plan. She had no medical insurance and wasn't eligible under Frank's insurance. Dolores would never receive any part of Frank's social security income, and, of course, she couldn't even apply for alimony. Legally, Dolores and Frank were considered strangers.

If Dolores and Frank had lived in one of the few states that recognize common-law marriage, Dolores could have attempted to prove that such a marriage existed. The states that recognize common-law marriage are: Alabama, Colorado, Georgia, Idaho, Iowa, Pennsylvania, Rhode Island, South Carolina, and Texas; the District of Columbia also recognizes common-law marriage. In any state, however, common-law marriage is difficult to prove. Obviously, there is usually little or no documentation to support your claim that an informal marriage existed. Although each state has its own requirements, the law generally requires that you prove two elements to establish a common-law marriage:

1. An agreement between the parties to be married.

Regardless of how long you and your partner have lived together, the court must find that you and your partner entered into an agreement providing that you would consider yourselves to be husband and wife. While it is not required that the agreement be in writing, you must have supporting evidence to prove that an agreement existed. Did you hold a private ceremony? If so, can you establish where and when it took place? Did you ever promise each other that you would be together forever and would treat each other as husband and wife? Perhaps there are love letters or birthday, anniversary, or holiday cards which contain a note to this effect. If you have no supporting documentation, the court hearing may come down to your word against his.

2. Representing yourselves as husband and wife to the world.

Have you or your partner referred to the other as "spouse" or "husband" or "wife" in front of friends, family, or others? If so, your argument that an informal marriage existed will have credibility. Did you ever apply for a mortgage or loan as husband and wife or sign any legal papers as husband and wife? Did you ever draw up wills which made it clear that you considered yourselves married to each other? The testimony of third parties showing that they believed a "marriage" existed between you and your partner may be required to establish this element to the court.

Palimony

At this point you're probably saying, "Wait a minute. I've heard about palimony. Michelle Marvin got palimony from Lee Marvin. Why can't I get palimony?"

Everyone remembers the infamous California case involving the actor Lee Marvin. Michelle Triola Marvin (she changed her name to Marvin) argued that she was entitled to support and a division of property from Lee Marvin when he left her, although they had never been legally married. What most people don't remember is that Michelle won the battle but lost the war. The California court decided it had the power to divide the property of this unmarried couple according to their reasonable expectations, but found that Michelle couldn't prove the elements necessary to establish her right to a portion of Lee Marvin's property. In the end, she received nothing.

Although much heralded at the time, the Marvin case is now fifteen years old and has not had much of an impact. While recognized in California, other courts throughout the United States have held that palimony is not valid and that only those legally married will be entitled to spousal rights. Clearly, you should not expect palimony if your living-together arrangement terminates. However, if you are unmarried and living with your partner, there are steps you can take to provide you with the legal protection you need.

Cohabitation Agreements

As you have already seen, prenuptial agreements are valid legal documents that can provide for certain spousal rights agreed upon by the parties, regardless of what the law calls for. The same type of contract can be drawn between two unmarried persons to confer rights that they would not otherwise have had. Like prenuptial agreements, cohabitation agreements might not be for everyone. In addition, they are not considered valid in every state. However, such an agreement may be the only way to protect your property rights if the relationship ends. Consider entering into such an agreement if:

1. You have lived with your partner for over six months.

Over 20 percent of couples who cohabit will live together for five years or more. The longer you live together, the more likely it is that you will purchase property or accumulate other assets which must be divided if the relationship ends. Also, chances are that certain debts will arise, such as charge-card debt, which you don't want to get stuck with alone if both you and your partner are responsible.

2. If you own real estate.

You and your partner should enter into a written agreement *before* any real estate has been purchased. However, if you have already purchased real estate, see a lawyer immediately. The sooner you obtain a written agreement which divides the property if you break up, the more secure you'll be.

3. When there are children.

Children born to spouses during a legal marriage are presumed to be the children of the spouses. However, no such legal presumption exists if you are unmarried. To prevent problems regarding the paternity of your children, a cohabitation agreement can state that your partner acknowledges the children are his and that he is financially responsible for them.

Although you and your partner could write an informal cohabitation agreement yourselves, I strongly recommend that you have an attorney draft your cohabitation agreement. The contract does not have to be complicated or lengthy. It can include everything from simple matters, such as who gets the Christmas decorations when you split, to the more significant issues, such as how the real estate will be divided and who will become responsible for any outstanding bills.

Cohabitation agreements are not valid in all states. Consequently, speak with an attorney in your area about such an agreement. If your state recognizes these contracts, entering into such an agreement may be the only way to avoid being shortchanged when the relationship ends.

Joint Property vs. Individual Property

Most women who live with a partner do not have cohabitation agreements protecting their property rights. In such cases, you may wonder what will happen to your assets (and debts) when you and your partner split. If there is no written agreement, all property will be divided depending upon how title is held when the relationship ends. Is the checking account in his name? What about the car? What if he leaves without paying you for his share of the monthly bills? Which party becomes responsible for the debts and which party receives the assets depends upon whose name is legally attached to these items.

As a general rule, men are more aware of whose name property is titled in, and usually title property in their own name. Unfortunately, in many situations women defer to the man's preference for holding title in his name, wrongly believing that the issue is more an emotional one than a legal one.

For example, your partner might encourage you to deposit your checks into his bank account, saying, "Honey, you know the money belongs to both of us. The bank will just make us do a lot of paperwork to change the account into both of our names, and might even charge a fee. Don't you trust me?"

Women involved in these relationships must be aware of how title to all property is held and how it will affect them if they split with their partner. There are basically three forms of ownership which you must be aware of in order to protect your property rights.

1. Sole ownership

Sole ownership is the simplest form of legally owning property. It means that only one person has legal title to an asset. For example, if your car is registered in your name alone, you have sole ownership of this asset. If your partner were to terminate the relationship, the car would legally remain yours—unless a contract provided otherwise or unless a common-law marriage was established. As a general rule, when an asset is solely owned, no other person has legal rights to that asset.

If you really want to protect your property, and make sure that what's yours stays yours, title the asset in your name alone. That way, it will be difficult, if not impossible, for your partner to claim an interest in that asset.

2. Joint ownership—joint tenancy

Joint tenancy is the most common way that two people own an asset together. Many married couples hold assets as joint tenants. When you and I own property as joint tenants, we are each entitled to 100 percent of the asset. For example, if we have a savings account which lists both our names as joint tenants, we both own all of the money in that account. This means that either of us may withdraw all the money in that account—not just 50 percent—without the consent of the other joint tenant.

A major advantage of joint tenancy is the "right of survivorship." This right provides that when one of the joint tenants dies, the other joint tenant automatically becomes entitled to all interest in the asset—even if a will states otherwise. Consequently, I would be entitled to keep all of the money in that joint savings account no matter what your will says.

3. Joint ownership—tenancy in common

Tenancy in common is another method of owning property when more than one person is involved. It is similar to joint tenancy, except for two differences. As tenants in common, we each own a specific percentage of the asset. For example, if we have a bank account as tenants in common, we each own 50 percent or some other specific percentage. Unlike joint tenants, we don't each have 100 percent rights to the account. Because of this difference, there is no right of survivorship. If you should die owning the asset with your partner, your share will pass to your heirs by will or according to the law of your state if there is no will. However, it will not automatically pass to the other tenant in common, as it would under joint tenancy.

It is essential that you determine how your assets are held.

When your relationship dissolves, your partner is legally entitled to all property held in his name and held in joint tenancy with you. Protect yourself by having all property that is considered yours held individually in your sole name, without any form of ownership in your partner's name. If you wish to hold certain property jointly, ask yourself whether the property should be held in joint tenancy or in tenancy in common. If you and your partner own property as tenants in common, property you thought might pass to you in the event of his death may not, if he has a will that provides otherwise or has no will at all.

Consult with an attorney to determine the best method of holding title to all property.

Who Owns the House?

For most of us, the largest financial investment we will ever make is the purchase of a home. Although you may not marry, chances are good that you and your partner will buy property together or that you may contribute to the upkeep of property owned by the other. However, such a seemingly happy and simple event can easily turn into a nightmare.

The case of Mr. Smith illustrates what can happen to women when they enter into such a major financial commitment without being aware of the ramifications. One month after Smith began living with his partner, he suggested that they build a new home, which they would pay for together. Title was taken in his name solely, but he promised to transfer title to both of their names as joint tenants. Smith also agreed that his partner would receive half of the house if they broke up.

Smith and his partner lived together for twelve years. During several of those years, Smith was unemployed and so his partner made the payments on the house herself, including paying the taxes and insurance. When they broke up, his partner found out that Smith had never put her name on the title. Unfortunately, though, her name was on the mortgage. As a result, she was responsible for continuing to pay the mortgage but was not entitled to any share of the value of the house.

This true case illustrates why you should *never* enter into any agreements regarding real estate without consulting an attorney. The most typical problems that arise between unmarried couples involve real estate. Women tend to be all too trusting and allow a virtual stranger to take control, and even to take possession, of their property. A common scenario that lawyers see these days involves a man moving into a woman's house. Often, the woman received the home in a divorce settlement. When she lets her new partner move in, he agrees to pay half the mortgage and the other expenses. In exchange, he wants his name on the title to the property. Believe it or not, some women agree to this, thinking that since he's paying half of the costs, it's only fair that his name should be put on the title to the house. It's when they break up or the house is to be sold that the woman suddenly understands what happened—she gave away one half of *all* the interest in the house. The problem is that her partner never paid anything in the years before he moved in and never contributed to the down payment. While he should receive the money he put into the house, he shouldn't be entitled to one half of the entire value. Yet by putting his name on the title as a joint tenant, you have just given him a huge windfall—at your expense.

The Smiths of the world take advantage of unsuspecting women who become financially and emotionally obligated— never caring about the tragic consequences that might follow. Before you become legally responsible for the payment of thousands of dollars, or consent to your partner's living in your home, call your lawyer. Make sure that your rights to the property are protected.

What About the Children?

Mothers who have had children with their live-in partners often ask what rights they have if the father leaves and refuses to pay support. Although this subject will be considered at length in Chapter 11, you should know that children born "out of wedlock" are considered equal to those born within a marriage. Regardless of whether you married the father of your child, you may pursue an action for paternity to establish his legal obligations to the child. Once paternity is proven, the father is legally recognized as the biological parent. He will be required to pay child support and make other financial contributions, and he becomes entitled to rights of visitation and, perhaps, custody.

You can see why many people argue that women should never live with a partner "without benefit of marriage." When these relationships end, women are the real losers. They are left with no legal rights and no recourse. There are no financial or legal benefits to living together—no alimony, retirement plan, social security, or medical insurance and, perhaps, no home. Remember, there is only one way to be assured of having the benefits awarded to spouses—that is, having a legal marriage.

Gay/Lesbian Couples

Legal marriages between same-sex couples are not yet recognized in the United States. However, some cities are beginning to allow gay and lesbian couples some of the benefits of marriage by permitting them to obtain a legal certificate recognized by the city. For example, a New York and Los Angeles grant permits members of same-sex couples paid leave in the event of the death or sickness of their partner, if they can establish the existence of their relationship and the requisite duration of the relationship.

Since gay and lesbian couples may never be entitled to the benefits of marriage, a cohabitation agreement is essential to ensure the legal rights and responsibilities which each partner wishes to have.

Chapter 11

And Baby Makes Two— Paternity in the 1990s

Women in increasing numbers are choosing to have children without being married. Statistics show that one out of every four babies in this country is born out of wedlock. While most of these young women are poor and uneducated, the biggest increase in unwed mothers is among professional women in their thirties. These middle-class working women are opting not to marry but yet to have children. The growing societal acceptance of single mothers accounts for much of the increase. Women who are in their thirties or even forties find that their biological clocks are ticking but often can't find a man worth marrying. As a result, many women are choosing to become single mothers.

Since the stigma attached to having a child out of wedlock has all but disappeared, the law no longer uses the label "illegitimate" to describe these children. The law now mandates that children born to unmarried parents have the same legal rights as children born during a marriage. However, before a child can be afforded those rights, you must first establish the paternity of the child.

Unfortunately, some women choose to avoid this legal procedure. Frequently, mothers believe that they don't need financial assistance from the father and can raise the child just fine without his help. While this may be possible, the choice of many independent women to go it alone could shortchange the child. Events may occur that you didn't expect when you made the decision to forgo a paternity suit. What happens if you suddenly lose your job or your child is diagnosed with a serious illness or disability? Overnight, you may find that financial assistance from the father is crucial to the well-being of the child. In addition to the financial benefits of establishing paternity, there are other, less tangible benefits. One day your child may wish he had been acknowledged by his father—whether for emotional reasons or other reasons.

Some women deliberately avoid a legal action against the father, thinking that he will have no rights to custody or visitation if paternity and child support are not pursued. As will be seen, this incorrect assumption can cause you and your child to go without the financial assistance to which the child is entitled and will not protect you from an action by the father if he decides to pursue a relationship with the child.

Establishing fatherhood. Should I sue for paternity?

In order for your child to receive any legal or financial benefits from his father, you must legally establish the paternity of the child. If the father won't voluntarily admit to paternity, it will be necessary for you to bring a lawsuit against him to prove his parentage and to obtain child support and other benefits to which your child would be entitled. In deciding whether you wish to pursue such a case, be aware of the pros and cons involved in going to court.

The advantages of establishing paternity are:

- Your son or daughter becomes entitled to child support until he or she reaches age eighteen, and to the other benefits that any child would receive if his parents divorced, such as medical insurance and educational costs.

- Your child will be considered a legal heir of the father and will have rights of inheritance. In addition, the child becomes entitled to certain benefits at the father's death, including life insurance, social security, and perhaps veteran's benefits.

- You may be reimbursed for the medical costs of your pregnancy and for attorney's fees.

- The child has a chance to develop a relationship with the father and with the other half of his biological family.

Most women who find themselves facing this dilemma say the biggest risk they take is that the father may retaliate by involving himself in the child's life in a negative way. Another disadvantage is that you may not obtain child support if the father is unemployed or if he skips town to avoid paying.

While the unpleasantness of a court battle and the other

disadvantages must be considered, I have found that women give up on paternity all too quickly. They fall for the typical threats: "You'll be sorry if you sue me. I'll drag in every guy you've ever slept with." In many cases the man admits that he is the biological father (more about this later). As with any other court battle, you might have a tough road ahead of you. However, when paternity can be established, your child will be the winner in the long run. Even if the father can pay nothing now, your child will have a claim against him if he should come into some money in the future. In addition, the child-support obligation survives past the father's death and your son or daughter will have a claim against the father's estate. Even if the father receives only unemployment compensation, the court will require that some amount of what he receives go toward child support. Since we never know what the future may hold or who will win the lottery, it doesn't hurt to establish paternity and have a child-support order entered.

The question of whether to pursue a paternity case may be academic if you have received public aid since the birth of your child. All states have agencies that are required to pursue paternity on behalf of a child if the state has made payments to you for the child. If you have received assistance from the state, you must give your caseworker the name of the father or the names of possible fathers. Failure to cooperate could result in the loss of benefits. Take advantage of the state's program to pursue paternity and provide as much information as they need to prove that the defendant is the father of your child. You will avoid the necessity of hiring and paying for a lawyer, and will obtain benefits for your child, including the benefit that he has been legally acknowledged by his father.

I want to sue for paternity—how do I start?

Once you have chosen to fight for your child's rights, you must decide whether to hire a private lawyer or to use the state's attorney's office. Most women are not aware that the state will provide an attorney free of charge to pursue parentage matters. It is not necessary that you receive public assistance or that your income fall below a certain amount. The law considers it to be in the public interest to determine the parentage of all children, regardless of the income of the mother. Of course, a lawyer whom the state assigns to you usually has hundreds of cases to deal with, so you might wish to hire a private attorney to represent you and your child.

The father says he'll admit paternity—do we have to go to court?

One of the first questions your lawyer will ask is whether the child's father might admit to paternity. Many fathers acknowledge their paternity voluntarily—although perhaps not until the court papers have been filed. Once you've called his bluff, very often the father does not want to go through the cost and embarrassment of a trial any more than you do, especially if he is married or is a respected person in the community. If you are using the state's attorney to prosecute him, he knows that it is not costing you a dime but he must pay out of his own pocket to defend the case. In addition, he may not be anxious to be cross-examined in court by your lawyer about his past.

If the father agrees to admit his paternity, the procedure is quite simple. He signs a written document, under oath, stating that he is the father. This document is then filed with the court and it forever acknowledges his paternity of your child. Once this step has been completed, the court can determine the amount of child support and other financial assistance which he must provide. As with a divorce case, the child-support pay- ments might be taken directly from the father's paycheck and sent to you.

One of the primary reasons why some women decide against a paternity action is that they don't want the father to have contact with the child. However, once it is established that the man is the biological father, the law entitles him to rights of visitation—unless you can prove that visitation would not be in the child's best interests. There are many ways of demonstrating that visitation may not be appropriate. For ex- ample, if the father cannot adequately care for the child, the court will restrict or preclude visitation. This is likely to be the case with an infant or young child. Reasons that would cause the court to withhold visitation entirely include substance- abuse problems on the part of the father, previous charges of child abuse, neglect, or abandonment, or any facts demonstrat- ing that the father is unfit.

Women frequently ask whether visitation will be restricted if the father refused to acknowledge paternity and put her and the child through the ordeal of a long paternity trial. Believe it or not, in most cases the father's denial will have no effect on his rights of visitation. The law allows the father to deny pater- nity and demand that you prove your case to the court. How- ever, once proven (even over his denial), a biological parent has the constitutional right to participate in the life of the child. Consequently, the court will establish a visitation schedule, un-

less you and the father agree on one yourselves or you prove
that visitation should be restricted or withheld.

The father says he'll just deny it. What about blood tests?

If the father will not admit paternity, you have no choice but to
take the case to trial. It will be your job to prove to the judge or
jury that the defendant is the biological father of your child. To
support your case, you may present any relevant evidence.
However, these days paternity cases are basically decided on
one piece of evidence—the blood test. This is another reason
why men often admit to paternity; they change their denial
when the blood test results come back positive.

Blood tests now determine the outcome of paternity cases
because scientific advances have made the results highly accurate. However, no test has yet been invented that can absolutely prove that a man is the father of a child—although scien-
tists claim they can do so with an accuracy of 99.9 percent. On
the other hand, a test can definitely prove that a man is not the
father of a child. When the results show that the defendant
cannot be the father, this is called an exclusion. When the
results show he can be the father, the defendant is included in
the group of possible fathers, whether the chances are 1 percent or 99.9 percent. Although the laws differ from state to
state, you will still have the opportunity to establish paternity,
regardless of whether the test shows a 50 percent probability or
a 99.9 percent probability. Until the experts invent a foolproof
test that can definitively establish paternity, the courts will be
required to rely on additional evidence to determine the parentage of a child.

Since the technology regarding these tests is quite complex and changes every day, each court has different rules regarding the types of blood tests that it will accept. Regardless of the other specifics of your test, make sure the test includes two important elements, HLA and DNA. In general, the more genetic markers that are checked, the greater the likelihood that the results will accurately establish paternity. A complete test may check for as many as ninety different genetic markers.

Obviously, there is more to these tests than simply comparing the blood types of the parents and the child. While most experts believe in the accuracy of these tests, some studies have disputed their reliability. Therefore your attorney must have a detailed understanding of the science involved in these tests to determine when certain results should be questioned or challenged.

Paternity tests can be expensive, costing approximately $250 per person. Since the mother, the child, and the alleged father must be tested, the total cost can be $750 or more for one testing. If either side disputes the results, the court might allow a second test to be conducted. Who pays depends upon the rules of the court and the finances of the parties. In some states, the mother must help pay for part or all of the test, unless she is receiving public assistance or the father is financially able to pay.

If the father disputes paternity and blood tests must be taken, follow these important steps:

1. Wait until the baby is at least six months old. Some experts question results taken before this age.

2. Don't appear for the test if you or the baby are ill or received a blood transfusion within the last six months. The test results might not be accurate.

3. Make certain that you and the father produce current photo identification and appear for the test at the same place and time. More than one father has attempted to have a friend appear in his place.

4. The testing facility should have you and the father sign a statement consenting to the test. Make sure he signs. If you are not present, handwriting analysis can confirm who really appeared.

5. The testing facility should have you and the father initial the seal that is placed over each tube of blood. Since the lab probably tests hundreds of samples each day, signing the tube should reduce the chances of a mix-up and provide another handwriting sample.

Be prepared for a surprise when the tests come back from the lab. The results may exclude the alleged father entirely or may include him as a possible father but not with as high a probability factor as you expected. If you know that this man is the father, ask your lawyer to petition the court for a second test. Even the most experienced labs have been known to make mistakes, and more than one woman has been shocked to receive results that dispute her claims regarding paternity.

What else can I do to prove paternity?

Many years ago, before complex blood tests were created, courts had to rely on other forms of evidence when the paternity of a child was questioned. For example, there was the "hold up the baby test." If the baby looked like the father, the jurors were inclined to say that paternity had been established.

We've come a long way since that time. However, until blood tests are 100 percent accurate and above reproach, courts will still look at other forms of evidence to establish that the defendant fathered the child in question. After you have completed all blood tests, consider other evidence you can present to the court:

- Your testimony concerning sexual relations with the father. State the specific dates, times, and places.

- Any written evidence you have concerning the intercourse that took place. Pages from your diary, a hotel register, restaurant receipts, or other evidence that you were with the defendant at the time in question.

- Evidence, including your testimony, that the father accompanied you to a physician or clinic to determine whether you were pregnant or for pre- or postnatal care.

- Gifts, both in cash and otherwise, which the father sent after he learned of the pregnancy, and particularly after the child was born.

- Purchase of baby books, including books for selecting a name for the child.

- Any evidence that the father considered the child his own. This includes testimony of friends or family that he called the child "my son" or "my daughter," placed the child on his health or life insurance policy, and sent out birth announcements.

- Any evidence that the father signed the birth certificate or other document stating that he was the father of the child.

You might be surprised to learn that this last element does not conclusively establish paternity. Courts have declined to find that a defendant fathered a child even when his name appeared on the birth certificate. Hospitals used to allow a woman to name the father of the child without requiring the consent or signature of the father. These days many hospitals require that the name of the father be left blank unless he signs a document acknowledging that he is the father and agreeing to have his name on the birth certificate. This document is only one piece of evidence that the court may consider, along with the blood-test results and all other relevant evidence.

Since it is important to have as much evidence as possible to bring to the court, you should file for paternity as soon as you can. In fact, the papers may be filed prior to the birth of the child. The father can be served with the court papers before the birth and the blood tests taken months later. The longer you wait, however, the greater the chance that evidence will be lost or destroyed, that witnesses may refuse to testify, or even that the father will be deceased.

States differ as to how much time you may have to file suit, but in many cases suit may be filed until the child is eighteen years old. If the mother and father are still living, a blood test can be conducted which will go a long way toward determining paternity. However, the fact that you didn't file suit years ago may be considered by the judge or jury if paternity has been denied and the blood tests were inconclusive. Nonetheless, don't discount the possibility of a suit simply because your child is no longer an infant. As a general rule, the blood tests will tell the real story—and the passage of time can't change the results of the tests.

The father says he'll drag my name through the mud if we go to trial. What rights do I have?

The typical defense of men sued for paternity is to claim the child is not theirs and that you had sexual relations with other men. Thankfully, many judges and jurors are less concerned about the morals of the mothers and more concerned about a man's accepting legal responsibility for his child. Unfortunately, though, men still attempt to attack the character of the mother by portraying her as someone who "sleeps around."

Talk candidly with your attorney about whether you had sexual relations with more than one man during the time of conception. Hiding this information will only backfire on you when your unsuspecting lawyer gets these facts thrown at him from the other side. If you aren't certain which man fathered your child, your lawyer may ask each of the candidates to submit to a blood test prior to filing suit. Paternity matters can be settled privately without the necessity of going to court if the parties are willing to submit to blood tests.

Over the years the law has become less willing to admit

evidence of the mother's sexual history. Today evidence of the mother's intercourse with others may not be admitted unless it occurred during the period of conception. Consequently, if you had sex with another man six months before your child was conceived, your attorney may ask that the judge prohibit the defendant from bringing this up at trial in any way, since it could not possibly be relevant to the paternity of your child.

I've heard that the father of the baby could bring a suit admitting paternity, and ask for custody or visitation rights. Is that true?

Yes, it is true. Biological fathers are entitled to file parentage suits in which they admit to being the father of a child and ask the court for custody or visitation rights. Of course, such situations occur very rarely. A man may also bring suit to prove that he is not the father, and request that blood tests be performed. However, fathers rarely file suit. If you find yourself defending one of these cases, determine whether the father is legally within the time to file suit and assess his chances of winning.

If the father does file suit for paternity, ask your lawyer whether his time for filing such a case has expired. While this may seem simple, the time for filing can actually be a complex legal matter. In some states, a father may file such an action for only a limited period, such as before the child is two years old. If he has filed after that time the case may be dismissed. In other states he may have until the child reaches age eighteen.

If he is within the time limitations, you must decide whether or not to stipulate that he is the biological father. Just because he admits to it doesn't mean he really is the father.

Some men form close attachments to children, and when the relationship with the mother ends, he may not want to relinquish control of the child. Talk with your lawyer about whether to request a blood test to confirm paternity.

Presuming that he is the father of the child, determine whether his request for custody or visitation is sincere or whether it is a tactic. For example, if you told him you were thinking of filing a paternity case, he may have decided to file first and request custody. He figured he would scare you into reducing child support so you could keep custody. As with any other request for custody or visitation, the court must determine what is in the best interests of the child. If you have been the primary caretaker of the child, or the only caretaker, the court is unlikely to give the father custody or even much visitation. When the child is of tender years, the court is still inclined to place custody with the mother and grant the father only such visitation as might be appropriate under the circumstances.

In paternity cases, however, a child may have had little to no contact with the father prior to the time the case was brought. A judge is not likely to place the child in the hands of someone whom the child doesn't know—even if he is the biological father. Visitation arrangements are often created which allow for very little contact initially, and perhaps only in the presence of the mother or an agreed-upon third party. As the child gets older the court may grant greater time to a father who has consistently kept up reasonable visitation without problems. Of course, custody is unlikely to be an issue in these cases unless the fitness of the mother is in question, which is rare.

Remember, once paternity has been established, the father

becomes entitled to visitation rights that have been established by the court or to which you have agreed. As a result, just as in a divorce case, you may not unreasonably withhold visitation. Should you do so, the father may petition the court to enforce his rights of visitation, and may ask that the court sanction you for your failure to abide by the visitation schedule. Such sanctions may include expansion of his rights of visitation or, in extreme cases, changing the custody arrangement previously entered into.

My boyfriend and I got married when I was pregnant with our baby. Now that we're divorcing, he says the child isn't his.

In many states a child born during or after a marriage is legally presumed to be a child of the spouses. In those cases the parent who is questioning paternity must obtain enough evidence to rebut the legal presumption that the parents of the child are the spouses. If your husband questions paternity of a child, the time for doing so is before the divorce becomes final. Several courts have held that a father cannot contest the parentage of children born after marriage unless he does so during the divorce proceeding. This may be true even if the father can later prove conclusively that the child is not biologically his.

I never filed for paternity and my child is now an adult. Can he file against his father?

In most states, your son can sue his biological father for paternity until his twentieth birthday. He would be required to produce the customary evidence, such as blood tests and any relevant testimony or documentation. Depending upon how the father has treated your child over the years, it may be easier or more difficult for your child to establish paternity years after his birth. If the father never acknowledged the child and had no contact with him, it will be a difficult case to prove, unless the blood tests show a very high probability of paternity. On the other hand, the father might have sent cards and letters over the years calling him "son" and perhaps told others in the family that he had a child. He may have supported the child for a period of time, and sent birthday and Christmas gifts. If paternity is established, your son becomes an heir of the father and may be entitled to past child support and other financial assistance.

A child's relationship with a parent may be the most important relationship of his life. Don't deprive your child of such a relationship lightly. Regardless of the feelings you have for your child's father, allow the best interests of your child to guide you in determining a suitable custody and visitation arrangement.

Chapter 12

It's Not Over—
Postdecree Court

For months and perhaps years you looked forward to the day you would march out of court with your divorce papers. Yet for most people, the trouble has just begun. Some people spend more time in postdecree court than they did in divorce court. This is where you will come to have a judge resolve all the issues that arise after the divorce has been entered. This includes anything from forcing your husband to turn over the property you were awarded in the divorce to issues involving custody and visitation of your children. What are your chances of ending up in postdecree court? Well, the statistics show that in any given year more postdecree cases may be filed than divorce cases.

If you have children, you are almost guaranteed to be back in court. Even if you and your ex have a good relationship, disagreements are bound to arise over something having to do with the children. For example, as time goes on, you're likely to want an increase in child support, since the costs of raising the children increase as they get older. On the other hand, your former spouse is likely to want a decrease in support. If he remarries and has another family, he'll expect to pay you less, because he now has other children to support. Lawyers used to tell clients that they would be tied together until their children reached eighteen and went out on their own. Since some state laws now impose a duty on parents to provide for college education, divorced spouses remain in each other's lives even longer.

Many women don't realize that they may need the court more after the divorce is over than before. When your ex refuses to stick to the visitation schedule or to pay you his share of the children's medical expenses, postdecree court is your answer. Don't be shy about returning to court—your former husband won't be. Men are very well aware of their rights in postdecree court. They know this is where they come to ask for a decrease in child support or to ask that your alimony be terminated because you obtained employment or remarried.

The following will explain how postdecree court works, when you can expect to be back in court after the divorce is final, and how to use postdecree court to your advantage.

Is there a postdecree court in every state?

Yes. The law recognizes that after your divorce is final, disputes are likely to arise between you and your former spouse which cannot be resolved without court intervention. Consequently, the divorce courts retain the right to issue rulings to resolve certain legal disputes.

By the time a problem occurs, however, you or your spouse

might have moved out of the state which granted your divorce. Of course, you would prefer to have a court in your current state hear the case, rather than return to the state which originally issued the divorce. Unfortunately, determining which state is the proper forum to resolve disputes is a complicated matter, and you must consult a local attorney to determine where your postdecree matter should be filed. In general, though, issues involving children will be heard in the state in which the children currently reside. For example, let's say that you and your children moved from New York to California. A year later their father wishes to obtain custody and files in a New York court. In a typical situation, New York would not accept the case, and your ex-husband would be required to come to California to have the matter decided.

Is there a time limit for filing a postdecree case?

No. You may return to court anytime after your divorce is final to have the court resolve issues involving the children or other matters arising from the final settlement agreement. Some people find themselves in postdecree court one month after their divorce was entered, whereas others don't return for five or ten years. You may be one of the fortunate few who never appear in postdecree court. However, particularly when there are children, many people find themselves coming back every couple of years, or even every few months.

Although there is no limit to the number of times you may file a postdecree case, you must have a genuine legal issue that requires the court's attention. The court will not hear matters that are not legal issues, but simply disagreements between the parties. Nor will the court stand for one party filing postdecree cases for the purpose of harassment.

How does my divorce agreement affect postdecree rulings?

The starting point for all decisions that a postdecree judge makes is your final divorce documents. This is true whether your divorce was resolved by mutual agreement or whether the case went to trial and the court issued a ruling. The postdecree judge is bound by the prior agreement or ruling and cannot change the terms of that prior decision. For example, let's say that the final agreement provided that your spouse would pay you $5,000 and he has failed to do so. When you file your postdecree case, the judge is required to enforce that provision and order your ex to pay you the money. The judge does not have the power to alter or amend that provision in any way.

However, when it comes to issues involving the children, the court may not be bound by the prior divorce documents. The following scenario is typical. Although you were originally awarded sole custody, years later your ex decides that he wants sole custody or at least joint custody. Is the court required to dismiss his case because you were awarded custody previously? No. He can petition the postdecree court to change the custody arrangement at any time, even if he agreed to give you sole custody.

Of course, just because he asks for a change doesn't mean the court will grant his request. When it comes to the children, the court is required to make decisions based upon their best interests, even if a prior ruling or agreement provided for a different result. This is because a change of circumstances might have occurred which indicates that the custody or visitation arrangement should be altered. Similarly, although the divorce agreement stated that your ex would pay only a certain amount for child support, you may petition the court for an increase. If the court determines that the increase is warranted, your ex may be ordered by the court to pay more than the original agreement provided.

There are many reasons for coming back into court after the divorce is final. If any of the following circumstances arise, consider filing a postdecree case, on behalf of yourself or your children.

You want the settlement agreement overturned.

A significant number of women who end relationships are so distraught that they'll accept any settlement just to get the divorce over with. They say, "I don't want anything, just get me out of this marriage," or "It's as much my fault as his that the divorce happened; he can have whatever he wants. I don't even care what I get." You should care. No matter how humiliated or defeated you are now, chances are you'll feel a lot differently in six months or a year when you realize that you've settled for nothing.

Did you sign an agreement that you now realize was not in your best interests? If so, you may be able to do something about it, if you act quickly. In many states, it may be possible to have the settlement agreement vacated if you file a petition with the court within thirty days of entry of the divorce. However, the court won't vacate the judgment just because you changed your mind. By signing the divorce papers you entered into a legal contract that the judge cannot overturn without substantial evidence. As a general rule you must show that you did not understand the import of your actions or were coerced into signing the document.

The court will ask the following questions before vacating a settlement agreement:

- Were you represented by an attorney? If not, this fact alone may cause the court to vacate the agreement. If so, your case will be much more difficult to prove. Even if your lawyer did not represent you as well as he should have, your only recourse may be to sue him for malpractice.

- Were you under the influence of alcohol or drugs when you signed? Many women who are emotionally distraught during the divorce are prescribed tranquilizers by their doctor. If you were using drugs or alcohol or both, your judgment have been sufficiently impaired to call into question your ability to sign the document.

- Were you threatened by your husband? If he had a history of violence or was out of control while the divorce was pending, he may have forced you to enter into the agreement. If he brought the document home for you to sign, without an attorney or notary being present, the judge is more likely to believe that you were forced to execute the document and he may vacate the agreement.

Each state has different laws about vacating settlement documents. Think carefully about the ramifications of trying to vacate the agreement before you make such an attempt. In most cases, vacating the agreement also means vacating the divorce. If so, you will still be considered married and your divorce case will have to begin all over again. If you don't believe you should be held to the terms of the contract, talk with a lawyer immediately about whether you have grounds to overturn the document and whether you are still within the necessary time period.

My husband was hiding assets during our marriage. Can I do anything now?

This is a situation that divorce lawyers hear about all the time. Six months after the divorce is final you find out that your ex has a fabulous new wardrobe and is driving around town in a new $40,000 car. Yet only a few months ago he was pleading poverty, claiming that he couldn't afford any maintenance and that you were lucky to get the minimum amount of child support. Was he stashing money? Of course. The question is whether you can prove it.

Fortunately, it is not as difficult as it once was to establish that your ex failed to disclose all assets during the divorce negotiation. States now have specific laws which require that you be informed of all assets during the divorce. If you can prove that he didn't tell you about all the cash or other property that existed, whether deliberately or not, you may be entitled to a percentage of the hidden asset. Also, it is common for attorneys to include provisions in settlement agreements stating that if hidden assets are later uncovered, the offending party must pay for all attorney's fees necessary to obtain those assets and must provide the innocent spouse with a share greater than 50 percent of the undisclosed assets.

Establishing a case might not be as difficult as you think. After all, your ex had to pay for the clothes and the car with something. If he purchased these items with cash, it may be possible for your lawyer to show that your ex couldn't have earned enough money after the divorce to pay for these items. Your ex may not be able to explain where all the money came from. If so, you can establish that he failed to disclose assets.

Talk with your lawyer about the likelihood of establishing that assets were not disclosed. Determine whether your divorce agreement or the law of your state entitles you to attorney's fees if you prove your case. Spending thousands on legal fees to get hundreds from your ex may not be financially sound—although it may be satisfying in other ways.

My ex got a huge salary increase. Shouldn't he pay more child support?

Some experts estimate that more than half of all postdecree matters involve just this situation—cases where fathers have received increases in pay, but haven't passed a share on to their children through child support. The general rule is that a father is required to pay a percentage of his income toward child support. If he receives a raise after the divorce is final, he usually has an obligation to tell you about the increase, so that you or your lawyer can calculate the correct amount of support he should pay. Of course, it is unlikely that he'll comply with the law and give you this information voluntarily. Chances are you'll find out about the raise through your children or from some third party, and will have to file a postdecree case to get your children's fair share of his raise.

Once you have your ex in postdecree court, these cases are often cut-and-dried. Your ex will be required to show evidence of how much he now makes, and the court then applies the proper percentage to the new amount, depending upon how many children you have. There are some situations, however, when the court won't automatically increase your child support because of his raise. This is likely to happen in two circumstances: when the father claims increased expenses, or maintains that further support isn't financially necessary.

The first circumstance involves your ex petitioning the court for a decrease in support after you have petitioned for an increase. This is a typical tactic intended to take the sting out of your demand for an increase. Your ex will claim that not only should you not receive a portion of his raise but the court should actually decrease the prior amount which he had been paying. He will argue that he now has greater expenses than he had at the time of the divorce and simply doesn't have enough money to go around. This is usually as a result of having children with his new wife.

Whether he can avoid the increase, or even get a decrease, depends upon the law of the state. In many states, the judge must look at the father's finances and balance the need to support children from a first marriage with the need to support children from a second or subsequent marriage. This complex and controversial issue is one that is strenuously debated in legal circles, and is known as the "first-family priority" problem. Some experts believe that support for a first family should never be decreased because of subsequent family obligations, since the earlier family should be the father's first priority and since he voluntarily created further financial obligations by choosing to have more children. On the other hand, courts cannot allow children to go hungry, even if they are from a second or third marriage. The law has not yet reached a consensus on how to deal with this complicated issue.

However, if your ex claims that his additional expenses don't allow for the increase you requested, or even require a decrease, counter his argument by showing your own expenses —for both you and the children. Every parent knows that as children get older, greater sums of money are needed to care for them. In addition, the cost of living goes up every year. Since your salary probably didn't increase the way your ex's did, you're not even keeping up with inflation. You may also have had unexpected expenses, such as for a broken furnace or a leaky roof, which make the need for an increase absolutely essential. In many cases there are expenses directly relating to a child which should not be borne by the mother alone. For example, if a child was diagnosed as having a learning disability or an illness which resulted in large medical or counseling bills, the mother should make those expenses known to the court and ask that the father contribute.

The second situation that makes obtaining a support increase problematic—when the father argues that the child simply doesn't need an increase in support—occurs when the mother is employed and making substantial income herself or when the father's base salary was so high to begin with that a percentage of that amount is still in excess of normal child support.

Of course, it is only in rare cases that we find a father with such a high salary, usually in cases involving celebrities, athletes, or professionals with extraordinarily high incomes. If the father makes a million dollars a year, for instance, child support in some states could theoretically be set at $200,000, if the court were to follow the standard guidelines. However, courts have held that where a child is receiving very high child support due to a father's unusual salary, the child is not necessarily entitled to an increase when the father gets a raise or earns additional income. As with other cases, the court will look to the needs of the child and the ability to pay to determine an appropriate amount.

This is also true when the father has argued that the income of the mother is sufficient to care for the child. Even in these cases, fathers are still required to make a financial contribution. Under the law both parents have a legal duty to support a child. Just because the mother earns enough income to care for the child doesn't mean that the father is off the hook. The father's support can be deposited into an account for the child's college and graduate school expenses, or into a trust fund, to be used by the child for the purchase of a home or for other expenses after graduation.

If your ex has received an increase, or if you have greater expenses now than when the divorce was entered, talk with your lawyer about filing a petition to increase child support.

I want to terminate my husband's rights to visitation or custody.

Chances are that sometime after your divorce either you or your ex will ask a postdecree judge to make the most dramatic change possible to the prior divorce agreement, by asking to alter the visitation or custody arrangement. There are countless reasons why parents petition for such changes. Often, former spouses disapprove of the lifestyle of the other and wish to prevent the children from living in a particular environment. In a recent case I handled, the mother wished to restrict the visitation rights of the father since he began living with a woman who was a drug user and had the AIDS virus.

Commonly, fathers wish to increase their visitation or threaten to ask for custody, particularly when the mother has requested more child support. The question of when the court will change visitation and custody arrangements is complex and varies from state to state. In general, though, a parent must show a "substantial change of circumstances" before a court will order a change in the custody and visitation agreements. Remember the phrase "What is, shall remain"? Courts are not inclined to make major changes in the lives of children unless substantial proof is present that such a change will be in the best interests of the child and that new and unexpected circumstances caused the parent to ask for the change.

If you are asking that the court restrict your ex's rights to visitation or to switch the custody agreement, you have the burden of proving that the children will benefit from such drastic action. The following issues typically arise in these cases:

• Lifestyle

Your ex lives with his girlfriend, and he has no intentions of marrying her. You disapprove because your children are young and their father has overnight visitation. Will the court terminate all visitation? Not unless there are extenuating circumstances, but the court will probably prohibit overnight visitation —at least until the children are older.

You may have other disputes with your ex's lifestyle that cause you to question his right to visitation or custody. For example, does your ex consistently leave the children with a sitter when he should be spending time with them himself? If so, you may have a sound basis for cutting back on his visitation.

• **Substance abuse**

Unfortunately, numerous cases come into postdecree court based upon charges of drug or alcohol abuse. In almost all these situations, the primary issue is whether the actions of the father placed the children in danger. For example, was he drinking and driving with the children in the car? If so, you have a strong case for limiting or precluding visitation. But if the children are too young to testify, your allegations alone may be insufficient to establish that a problem exists. If so, you must present the testimony of other witnesses or medical or employment records to establish that your ex has a substance-abuse problem. If you meet your burden of proof, the court will determine the extent to which the problem is likely to affect the children, and balance that against the right of the father to see his children. The judge may allow your ex to have no visitation at all until he kicks his problem, or permit your ex to have only supervised visitation.

• Physical/sexual abuse

Allegations of physical or sexual abuse made within the context of divorce cases have skyrocketed. Studies differ as to how often such allegations are proven, and men's rights lawyers argue that women often make unfounded claims for purposes of harassment. Nonetheless, courts take any such allegations very seriously. Of course, sufficient evidence must be demonstrated to prove the claim, and this is often difficult to do when very young children are involved.

Cases involving these allegations are rarely decided only on the testimony of the parents. Most often, courts will require the testimony of experts, such as physicians, psychologists, and psychiatrists, before granting an order to change custody or visitation. Courts differ as to whether testimony from the child will be required, especially when the child is young. If testimony is essential, the child may be able to tell his story in the judge's chambers, rather than in the open courtroom.

Clearly, if the allegations are proven, a court will be swift to restrict or preclude the father's visitation or custody. However, allegations of physical or sexual abuse should *never* be made for improper purposes, such as for legal maneuvering or revenge. Claims made in bad faith may result in a loss of custody, restriction of visitation rights, or other sanctions resulting from perjury. If you do suspect that any physical or sexual abuse has taken place, have your child examined by a qualified physician who specializes in abuse cases. Then discuss the situation with your attorney, who will assist you in determining whether there are sufficient grounds to petition the court for a reduction or termination of visitation.

Postdecree court exists to help you and your children. Use this legal avenue to protect yourself and your children after the divorce is final. Don't fall victim to the threats that custody will be taken away from you if you seek more for your children. They're entitled to more—and with the help of postdecree court, you can see that they receive it.

Chapter 13

Knowledge Is Power:
Ten Questions Your Husband
Probably Can't Answer
But You Can

Now that you've had an opportunity to review your rights and responsibilities in the divorce court, let's see how well you apply what you've learned in some simple situations. Take the following multiple-choice quiz and see how you do.

Question 1: Jill married Mark, a doctor, in 1980. During their marriage, all assets were held in Mark's name, since he preferred it that way. Mark tells Jill that he has fallen in love with his nurse and will be filing for divorce. He says he only wants what's his, which is everything in his name. What should Jill do?

A. Give Mark a quick divorce and let him take every-thing.

B. Ask for 50 percent of everything, regardless of whose name it's in.

C. Demand everything! He's been a jerk and now he'll have to pay.

D. Get the best lawyer in town and find out what you are legally entitled to.

If you chose D, you have learned the most important lesson of all. Don't make quick decisions when you're in emotional turmoil. Once Jill obtains good counsel, she'll know what the law entitles her to and what type of distribution would be fair to her.

Question 2: Kathy and Steve have been married for seven years. In the last few months, Kathy has noticed some changes in Steve. He's been moody and depressed, comes home late from work, and has lost weight. She's asked Steve what's wrong, but he said he's just been having some trouble at his job. Yesterday he told her that he closed one of their accounts to pay some bills. Kathy should:

A. Try again to talk to Steve about what's wrong.

B. Call Steve's friends and co-workers to find out what's up.

C. Make sure all the bills are paid and find out how much is in the bank.

D. Do all of the above.

Once again, D is the right answer. Something is certainly going on with Steve, and he isn't telling Kathy—although she should give him another opportunity to do so. Steve has exhibited many of the classic warning signs that are often a prelude to divorce. Of course, Steve may be having other problems, including job difficulties or substance-abuse problems. However, Kathy will never find out unless she begins investigating.

Question 3: Sean and Diane have had a basically good marriage—except for those times when Sean drinks. Although he's never actually hit Diane, he has shoved her around and once even threatened to "take care of her for good" if she didn't bring him more booze. Is Diane a victim of domestic violence?

A. No, because he hasn't really hit her yet.

B. Yes, but only because he shoved her.

C. Yes.

Diane is a victim of domestic violence. Sean has abused her physically and psychologically, by threatening her life. It is no defense that he was drunk at the time. Diane must recognize that the abuse is likely to escalate if she doesn't take action to stop the abuse. Whether she decides to divorce him now or wait, she can obtain a criminal or civil Order of Protection. She is entitled to leave the home, along with her children, without being guilty of abandonment.

Question 4: Diane takes your advice and leaves Sean, telling him she won't return until he gets treatment. Sean refuses, so Diane decides to begin divorce proceedings. Can Diane get a greater share of the marital property because of Sean's abusive behavior?

A. Yes, because he caused her so much anguish.

B. No, since his conduct probably isn't relevant to dividing their assets.

C. No, because they have only minimal assets.

D. Yes, because she'll have to pay for therapy.

The answer is B. State courts differ on the relevance of conduct in dividing assets. However, if there are children involved, Diane can present evidence of his behavior to show that she should receive custody and ask that his visitation rights be limited or terminated until he gets help.

Question 5: One year ago Mary filed for divorce from Sam, who has been dragging his feet about providing information regarding their assets. What can Mary's lawyer do to find out what assets exist?

A. Take Sam's deposition.

B. Subpoena their bank statements.

C. Subpoena the records of Sam's employer, including pension and profit-sharing records.

D. All of the above.

The answer, of course, is D. Even without Sam's help, Mary's lawyer can obtain a great deal of information, using the subpoena power of the court. If Sam refuses to disclose information at his deposition, Mary's lawyer can file a motion with the court asking that Sam be held in contempt for his failure to properly tender the necessary information.

Question 6:   In the final divorce agreement, Mike was required to pay off a Visa bill for $3,000 that was in both his name and Sharon's. Visa has now sued Sharon for that amount, since Mike stopped making the monthly payments. Who is responsible?

A. Under the terms of the divorce agreement, Mike is.

B. Sharon is responsible for half, since the bill was for things they bought while married.

C. Neither one. Since Mike has no money but should pay the bill, they can't make Sharon pay.

Technically, A is the correct answer. However, Visa may sue only Sharon if they wish, since her name was on the card also. Visa is not bound by the divorce agreement, but Mike is. Therefore, Sharon is entitled to bring Mike back to court to force him to pay the bill or to reimburse her for whatever she had to pay on his behalf.

Question 7: Nancy and Joe would both like custody of their two-year-old daughter, Elizabeth. Nancy worked as a schoolteacher until she had Elizabeth and has been at home since then. Joe has a job with flexible hours, so he can make his own schedule and often comes home for lunch. Although the marriage didn't work out, Joe and Nancy believe that Elizabeth's well-being is of the greatest importance. What type of custody arrangement would the court probably order?

A. Joint custody.

B. Joint parenting, with physical custody to Nancy.

C. Sole custody to Joe.

D. Sole custody to Nancy.

Were you stumped by this question? The answer is B. Considering all the facts, the court would probably lean toward giving both parents input into making decisions about Elizabeth's health, education, and welfare, but give physical custody to Nancy. Both parents obviously care for their daughter and seem willing to put their differences aside for her benefit. In addition, Elizabeth is very young and most courts would probably still prefer that she be with her mother. However, Joe is likely to receive very liberal visitation, even though the child is young, since he wants to be a coequal parent.

Question 8: Richard and Sally are at an impasse in their divorce negotiations. Sally does not believe that Richard has offered enough and thinks that she would get more if she went to trial. On the other hand, Sally would prefer to save herself the expense and aggravation of a trial. What are her options?

A. Sally could just agree to settle and take what he's offered. At least she'll be done with the whole thing.

B. Sally could do nothing and see if Richard changes his mind.

C. Sally could make a counteroffer.

D. Sally could ask for a pretrial.

Answers B, C, and D are correct. Sally should not get discouraged and accept just any offer. However, Richard may not want to wait either, and may decide to increase his offer just to get the divorce over with. If Sally makes a counteroffer, she might speed up this process. However, if nothing else works, Sally should have her lawyer request a pretrial. By learning the judge's recommendation, Sally can determine whether her request is out of line or whether Richard is being unreasonable.

Question 9: One week before they were married, Greg suddenly presented Judy with a prenuptial agreement. In the event of divorce, Judy would receive nothing from Greg, but in the event of death, Judy would receive one third of Greg's estate. Judy signed, since Greg said he wouldn't marry her otherwise. Greg was worth $5 million at the time of their marriage, and Judy had nothing. A year later, Greg sues Judy for divorce. What will she receive?

A. Absolutely nothing; she knew what she was doing when she signed the agreement.

B. Half of his $5 million, since the agreement is invalid.

C. Something, but who knows how much.

D. One third of his estate.

The answer is C. It would appear that the prenuptial agreement might be invalidated by the court. The agreement was presented one week before the marriage, with no prior discussion. Greg had substantial assets, but refused to give her anything regardless of how long they were married. Such a contract is unlikely to be upheld. However, even if invalidated, Judy is not automatically entitled to half of what Greg is worth. In fact, since the marriage lasted for such a short time, she is probably entitled to very little—but how much depends upon other facts and circumstances which only the court will be made aware of.

Question 10: Ron and Elissa lived together for three years and have a child, Tommy. When they split up, Ron refused to pay child support for Elissa, saying he's not really sure Tommy is his. What evidence is likely to be most persuasive to the judge?

A. The birth certificate, which Ron signed, saying he acknowledged being Tommy's father.

B. The blood tests showing a 95 percent chance that Ron is the father.

C. Testimony of Ron's family and friends that he admitted Tommy was his son.

D. All of the above.

While the court will consider all of this evidence in determining whether Ron is Tommy's father, the greatest reliance will be placed on the blood tests. However, in this situation it seems that all the facts establish that Tommy is Ron's child. Once the court enters such an order, Tommy will be considered Ron's child forever, including for purposes of inheritance.

You should feel very confident if you answered most or all of the questions correctly. Of course, real-life divorces tend to be messier and more complicated than hypothetical situations. Still, you should now realize that a little bit of knowledge can do a lot to even the odds.

Chapter 14

The Future of Family Law

If women increasingly assert their rights and the rights of their children—and if the courts support these rights—they may well occupy an equal or near-equal footing with their ex-husbands at some point in the future. But in the future other antagonists and situations may threaten those rights. Dramatic changes are occurring in the area of family law, and women should be aware of court decisions that may have a major impact on everything from custody to visitation. In addition, startling social trends are forcing the courts to consider more than the rights of each spouse. The rights of children, grandparents, stepparents, and others are now being blended into the legal mix.

Thirty years ago most people would not have believed that divorce would become an accepted part of our culture. Yet today, divorce is commonplace, and paternity cases are on the rise. What can we expect in the next twenty or thirty years? Consider just a few of the recent cases involving various areas of family law:

- In Tennessee, a judge granted custody to a father after the child's mother refused to give up cigarettes, despite the doctor's warning that secondhand smoke could harm her child. The appellate court upheld the decision, even after the mother stopped smoking.

- A hospital in Georgia accidentally switched two babies before sending the mothers home. Nine years later, when one set of parents was getting divorced, blood tests disclosed what had happened. The court refused to award custody to the child's biological family.

- After Hurricane Andrew hit Florida, parents "returned" a boy and a girl they had adopted the year before through the state. The adoptive mother claimed that the children were uncontrollable and threatened her biological children and that after the storm she could no longer care for them. The judge granted her petition to return the children to the state, over objections of the state's attorney that children cannot simply be returned after you've adopted them and taken them home.

Even family-law attorneys are surprised by situations such as these. However, such cases have given us a glimpse into the future of family law. The following predictions will show you where family law is headed and prepare you for the road ahead.

The Psychological Parent: When an Outsider Wants Your Child

One of the most important trends for the future of family law involves a concept called "the psychological parent." A psychological parent is someone who helped raise a child for a significant period of time and considers herself or himself to be a parent to the child—although there is no biological or legal relationship.

Women are increasingly involved in battles with former lovers, second husbands, and others who claim rights to children not their own. For example, a woman marries and she and her daughter live with her husband for six years. Although her spouse never adopts the child, he goes to court when the couple split, asking for visitation rights and a say in how the daughter will be raised. This situation has happened not only between heterosexual couples but also between gay partners. Should a woman's lesbian lover be entitled to custody or visitation rights regarding the lover's child?

This creative new theory goes against every legal doctrine that has been with us for generations. The law has always held that no one has rights to children greater than their parents, absent extraordinary circumstances, such as unfitness or neglect. This new psychological-parent idea challenges the very core of our laws as they relate to parental custody and control of children. However, as our society changes, eventually our legal system must do likewise. The reality is that many children live in households with persons they are not legally bound to and to a large degree are raised by that person and their parent. This troublesome issue will not disappear unless parents stop cohabiting and remarrying, and that is just not going to happen.

How do courts decide these cases? Perhaps surprisingly, some judges have continued to apply the "best interests of the child" standard used in divorce cases to determine the custody and visitation arrangements that would be most appropriate for a child. Some experts have argued that a different standard should be used in these situations—that is, the best interests of the family. They argue that what may be best for a child is not necessarily best for the family of that child, even if the "family" consists of divorced parents.

If you are living with another adult who is not the legal parent of your child, the adult may sue to retain involvement in your child's life, with or without your consent. Although these cases are still relatively rare, there are more and more situations where the psychological-parent theory has been raised. Until our legislatures pass new laws dealing with these situations, courts are likely to look at the same factors as in divorce cases.

A major question the court will ask is which adult has been the primary caretaker of the child. Who cooks the child's meals, spends the most time with the child, takes the child to school, etc.? The court may also consider other issues not present in divorce cases. For example, in many situations, a child is so young when the parents divorce that he has always referred to the new husband or male partner as "Dad." The more ties your child has to your partner, the more likely it is that the court may extend, at least, some visitation rights to your partner when the relationship ends. The stronger your own ties to your children, the less likely that a court will award rights to someone who is a legal stranger to the child.

Grandparents' rights

According to the 1990 census, over 3.3 million children live with their grandparents. And that's just the official figures. Many experts insist that this doesn't include the vast number of children who have informal living arrangements with their grandparents. There are many reasons why grandparents are more involved in the lives of their grandchildren than in former years, including the increasing divorce rate and the number of parents working outside of the home. Also, grandparents are living longer and are unwilling to give up their grandchildren simply because of a divorce or the death of a parent.

The "grandparents' lobby" is very strong. Today, almost every state has laws entitling grandparents to rights of visitation regarding their grandchildren. It often comes as a shock to parents that the grandparents' right to be with the child may override the contrary decision of the parent. This controversial law was adopted because it was believed that the relationship between grandparents and a grandchild is unique and that such a relationship is in the child's best interests.

Courts have been increasingly willing to provide grandparents with a greater role in the grandchild's life, regardless of the parent's feeling that such a role would not be beneficial to the child. Why have the courts taken such a generous stance toward grandparents? Remember, many judges sitting today are older and have grandchildren themselves. Judges often take the position that while the parent and the grandparents may not get along, allowing the grandparents visitation rights won't harm the child and may be a benefit.

Of course, if you have enjoyed a good relationship with your parents or your husband's parents, you will probably encourage your children to continue seeing their grandparents even after a divorce or the death of your spouse. However, not all families get along this well. You may have serious disagreements with the grandparents and concerns about your children being in their presence without your supervision. In fact, you may have limited their contact during your marriage.

If you are confronted with a petition for grandparents' visitation, you must prove to the court that such a relationship will have a negative effect on your children. Be assured that this will be very difficult to establish. Remember, the law guarantees grandparents these visitation rights already; it is your burden to prove why they should be denied these rights, and your dislike of the grandparents is not enough to overcome this burden. In some extreme cases you may be able to establish why they shouldn't see the children. For example, the grandparents may be alcoholics or physically or mentally incapable of caring for a child.

In almost all other cases the court is likely to fashion some type of arrangement, creatively avoiding the reasons for which you object. If there are religious differences between you and the grandparents, the court may order that visitation not take place during Christmas, Hanukkah, or other religious holidays.

If the grandparents live out of state, the court may decide that visitation take place at certain times so as not to disrupt the schedules of the children, such as during the summer or over spring break.

Whether grandparents can be awarded custody of a grandchild is a more complicated matter. Usually this issue arises only when both parents are deceased or have been found unfit. However, an interesting question is whether the rights of grandparents will one day extend to obtaining joint legal custody of grandchildren even while the parents are alive. As our society ages and the rate of divorce continues, it is probable that grandparents will seek to expand their legal rights to your children.

Children Who Divorce Their Parents

The Florida case of the twelve-year-old boy who successfully "divorced" his biological parents shocked both parents and those in the legal community. It represented a unique situation in which a child asked a court to sever all legal ties to his natural parents, notwithstanding the objections of the parents. Will this become a trend? Will children routinely go to court when their parents make decisions with which the children disagree?

Don't fear that your children will divorce you just because you wouldn't let them out to play or have that new pair of hundred-dollar sneakers. Although some have questioned how far the Gregory K. case might take us, it is very unlikely that this case will open the door to such frivolous and unwarranted claims. The rights of parents to control their children are still constitutionally protected and will not be denied lightly.

However, Gregory's case has established legal precedent for children in similar situations to bring actions to divorce their parents. Unfortunately, the sad story of Gregory's life isn't as rare as you might wish. According to court records, Gregory was passed from an abusive, alcoholic father to a neglectful mother, into a foster home, back to his mother, to another foster home, and then to a boys' ranch. Happily, Gregory finally ended up with a foster family that he grew to love and who loved him. They were successful in adopting Gregory as their ninth child, after the court found that Gregory had been neglected and abandoned by his natural parents. The court ruled it was in Gregory's best interests to remain with his foster family.

Critics argue that this case has established a dangerous precedent that threatens fundamental family principles. Some say that if children are allowed to divorce their parents, they will always choose parents who are more lenient and can provide more material possessions. Others say that Gregory's case has helped transform the legal view of children from being considered the property of parents to being human beings with their own rights.

Parents who are not abusive or neglectful and who care for their children have nothing to worry about. For those other children who are not so lucky, the law has now provided an alternative. However, until children can obtain, hire, and pay for attorneys, this legal solution may not be available.

Surrogacy

It has been five years since Mary Beth Whitehead attracted worldwide attention by refusing to turn over custody of a child she had borne as a surrogate mother. As you may recall, the court ultimately granted custody of the child to the natural father and his wife, but gave Ms. Whitehead rights of visitation. Since then, many states have restricted the practice of surrogacy. Today eighteen states strictly limit a woman's right to contract to carry a child and then transfer custody to the biological father and his wife.

Even so, many couples have decided that their only hope of having a child is through surrogacy. By some accounts, over 4,000 babies have been born in the United States through surrogacy arrangements. The couple and the surrogate sign a complicated contract which includes provisions regarding the fees paid to the surrogate and what happens if the child is born with a physical or mental defect or if the surrogate has twins. In some states, the practice of surrogacy is legal, except that no fees may be paid to a surrogate or to the broker who brought the parties together.

Opponents of surrogacy say that babies should not be sold, like commodities, and that the practice should be abolished. Others argue that laws banning or restricting surrogacy are anti-feminist, preventing women from doing as they choose with their own bodies. Most parents who contract with surrogates argue that they are not paying for a baby, but for the time and expenses of the surrogate. Women who act as surrogates often say that money has little or nothing to do with their decision; they have enjoyed the experience of being pregnant and wish to help a childless couple have a family of their own.

The surrogacy battle is far from over. Statistics show that the number of couples unable to conceive is increasing, and while traditional adoption might be possible for some, many believe surrogacy is the only alternative. One thing is clear: Situations involving surrogacy are becoming more complex. Recently a fifty-three-year-old woman in New York acted as a surrogate for her son and his wife and gave birth to her own grandson. How will the law deal with the complex and unexpected situations that arise? What happens if the surrogate has twins and will only surrender one of the children? What if she decides to give up the child for adoption? Clearly, the courts will be called upon to answer the myriad of questions for many years to come.

The Future of Divorce Court

The trend toward increasing numbers of divorces and remarriages is undeniable. On average, 50 percent of all marriages end in divorce and a staggering 80 percent of all divorced people remarry. By some accounts your chances of divorcing are greater after a second marriage than after a first. While it was once thought that the high rate of divorce would result in a decrease in remarriages, just the opposite has occurred. The practice of marrying, divorcing, and remarrying now has a name. "Serial monogamy" is here to stay. This trend escapes no age group, race, or religion. As our population is aging, we have found that divorce is especially increasing among older Americans. Divorcing at sixty and older is becoming a more common occurrence, as evidenced by divorce support groups for elderly Americans.

What lies ahead for those divorcing in the next century? I believe that the process must change to accommodate the increasing numbers of people who will go through the doors marked "Divorce Court"—perhaps more than once or even more than twice. The system has become unworkable and burdensome for the courts, for the lawyers, and for the clients. The future of divorce law lies in the area of alternative dispute resolution, also called ADR or mediation. ADR comprises a group of alternative procedures, other than traditional courtroom litigation, that people can use to resolve their disputes. Taking divorce out of the courtroom and into the hands of a private mediator will forever alter how millions of people obtain a divorce.

The advantage of mediation lies in the saving of time, money, and therefore aggravation for everyone involved. Litigation has become too expensive for most people. In major metropolitan areas, a typical divorce can take three to five years to resolve. Because of the time required, attorney's fees are staggering, running into tens of thousands of dollars. Clearly, the system is not working for the clients.

The legal community is also interested in finding an alternative to litigation. You may ask what motivates lawyers, since they are paid for their time. In truth, very often lawyers never receive the fee to which they are entitled. In many cases a lawyer cannot be paid until the case is resolved and the assets sold. However, by the time the case is resolved, the clients may have dissipated the funds or simply refuse to pay because they are unhappy with the process and with the result.

Clearly, everyone involved in the divorce system wants to find another option. ADR provides just that. There are different forms of ADR, including arbitration and mediation. Basically the parties and their attorneys agree to have the dispute resolved by an impartial third party outside of a courtroom. This might be a former judge, lawyer, or other professional trained in dispute resolution. The parties may agree in advance that they will be bound by the decision or, instead, that either party may disagree and only then proceed to court.

ADR is a recognized way of reducing the cost and the delay of litigation and is gaining in popularity as more judges and lawyers encourage its use. This form of resolving disputes will be especially beneficial to women (and children), who typically can't afford legal costs or long-drawn-out court cases. The courtroom, however, will never disappear. Some litigants won't agree to use ADR or to be bound by the mediator's decision, seeing it as an infringement of the constitutional right to their "day in court."

Until ADR becomes a widespread reality, women and children must continue to fight for their rights. Although it's been an unfair fight, women who understand the legal system and put that knowledge to use will have the ability to get what they and their children are entitled to.

Appendix A

Women's Bar Associations

Alabama

Mobile Bar Association
Women Lawyers Section
P.O. Drawer 2005
Mobile, AL 36652
205-433-9790

Alaska

Anchorage Association of Women Lawyers
P.O. Box 104971
Anchorage, AK 99510
907-278-6024

Arizona

Arizona Women Lawyers Association
1940 E. Thunderbird Road
Suite 103
Phoenix, AZ 85022
602-482-1827

Arkansas

Arkansas Association of Women Lawyers
P.O. Box 95
Little Rock, AR 72203-0095

California

California Women Lawyers
926 J Street, Suite 820
Sacramento, CA 95814
916-441-3404

Colorado

Colorado Women's Bar Association
1801 Broadway #350
Denver, CO 80202
303-298-1313

Connecticut

Connecticut Bar Association
Women and the Law Section
101 Corporate Place
Rocky Hill, CT 06067
203-721-0025

Delaware

Delaware State Bar Association
Section on Women and the Law
902 Market Street
Suite 1300
Wilmington, DE 19889
302-655-5000

District of Columbia

Women's Bar Association of DC
1819 H Street NW
Suite 1250
Washington, DC 20006

Florida

Florida Association for Women Lawyers
P.O. Box 10617
Tallahassee, FL 32302

Georgia

Georgia Association for Women Lawyers
999 Peachtree Street NE
Atlanta, GA 30309-3996
404-853-8298

Hawaii

Hawaii Women Lawyers
P.O. Box 2072
Honolulu, HI 96805

Idaho

Idaho Women Lawyers, Inc.
P.O. Box 1683
Boise, ID 83701

Illinois

Women's Bar Association of Illinois
321 South Plymouth Court
Suite 4S
Chicago, IL 60602
312-341-8530

Indiana

Indianapolis Bar Association
Women Lawyers Division
P.O. Box 2086
Indianapolis, IN 46206-2086
317-269-2000

Iowa

Iowa Organization of Women Attorneys
P.O. Box 65852
West Des Moines, IA 50265

Kansas

Wichita Women Lawyers
Wichita Bar Association
700 Epic Center
301 North Main
Wichita, KS 67202
316-263-2251

Kentucky

Kentucky Bar Association for Women
2700 Citizens Plaza
Louisville, KY 40202
502-589-5235

Louisiana

Louisiana Association for Women Attorneys
1126 Whitney Bank Bldg.
228 St. Charles Avenue
New Orleans, LA 70130
504-525-8832

Maine

Maine State Bar Association
1 Monument Square
Portland, ME 04101
207-773-6411

Maryland

Women's Bar Association of Maryland
WBA-MD State Bar Center
520 East Fayette Street
Baltimore, MD 21201
410-528-9681

Massachusetts

Women's Bar Association of Massachusetts
25 West Street
4th Floor
Boston, MA 02111
617-695-1851

Michigan

Women Lawyers Association of Michigan
P.O. Box 26245
Lansing, MI 48909-6245
517-487-3332

Minnesota

Minnesota Women Lawyers, Inc.
513 Nicollet Mall
Minneapolis, MN 55402
612-338-3205

Mississippi

Mississippi Women Lawyers Association
P.O. Box 862
Jackson, MS 39205-0862

Missouri

Association of Women Lawyers of Greater Kansas City
P.O. Box 414557
Kansas City, MO 64141

Montana

State Bar of Montana
Women's Law Section
P.O. Box 577
Helena, MT 59624
406-442-7660

Nebraska

Nebraska State Bar Association,
Women and the Law Section
P.O. Box 81809
635 S. 14th Street
Lincoln, NE 68501-1809
402-475-7091

Nevada

Northern Nevada Women Lawyers Association
350 S. Center Street #530
Reno, NV 89501
702-322-8999

New Jersey

New Jersey Women Lawyers Association
1200 Laurel Oak Road
Suite 100
Voorhees, NJ 08043
609-627-4954

New Mexico

New Mexico Women's Bar Association
P.O. Drawer 887
Albuquerque, NM 87103
505-842-8255

New York

Women's Bar Association of the State of New York
245 Fifth Avenue
Suite 2103
New York, NY 10016
212-889-7813

North Carolina

North Carolina Association of Women Attorneys
P.O. Box 28121
Raleigh, NC 27611-8121
919-833-4055 x34

Ohio

Greater Cincinnati Women Lawyers Association
P.O. Box 3764
Cincinnati, OH 45201-3764

Oklahoma

Oklahoma Association of Women Lawyers
Oklahoma Supreme Court
State Capitol
Oklahoma City, OK 73105
405-521-2163

Oregon

Oregon Women Lawyers
P.O. Box 40393
Portland, OR 97240
503-775-9021

Pennsylvania

NBA Women Lawyers Division
Philadelphia Chapter
P.O. Box 58004
Philadelphia, PA 19103

Rhode Island

Rhode Island Women's Bar Association
55 Dorrance Street
Providence, RI 02903
401-331-3800

Tennessee

Tennessee Lawyers' Association for Women
P.O. Box 2813
Nashville, TN 37219

Texas

State Bar Association of Texas
Women and the Law
P.O. Box 12487
Capitol Station
Austin, TX 78711
512-463-1463

Utah

Women Lawyers of Utah, Inc.
University of Utah, College of Law
Salt Lake City, UT 84112
801-581-4661

Vermont

Vermont Bar Association Women's Section
P.O. Box 100
Montpelier, VT 05601
802-223-2020

Virginia

Virginia Women Attorneys Association
2nd & Franklin Street
Suite 405, Linden Tower
Richmond, VA 23219
804-775-2431

Washington

Washington Women Lawyers
P.O. Box 25444
Seattle, WA 98125-2344
206-622-5585

Wisconsin

Association for Women Lawyers
777 E. Wisconsin Avenue
Milwaukee, WI 53202
414-289-3534

Appendix B

Income and Expense Affidavit

	Actual Monthly as of
	_____

A. Statement of Income and Deductions

    1. Gross Income per Month

        a. Salary/wages $_____

        b. Draw   _____

        c. Bonus   _____

        d. Pension   _____

        e. Annuity   _____

        f. Social security   _____

        g. Dividends   _____

        h. Interests   _____

        i. Trusts   _____

        j. Public Aid   _____

        k. Workmen's compensation _____

        l. Unemployment compensation _____

        m. Rents   _____

        n. Disability payments   _____

    o. Stocks   _____

    p. Bonds   _____

    q. Other (specify) _____   _____

Total Gross Monthly Income $_____

2. Required Deductions

    a. Taxes: federal (based on __ exemptions) $_____

    b. Taxes: state (based on __ exemptions)   _____

    c. Social security (or pension equivalent)   _____

    d. Mandatory retirement contributions required by law or as a condition of employment   _____

    e. Union dues   _____

    f. Health/hospitalization insurance   _____

    g. Prior obligation of support actually paid pursuant to court order   _____

    h. Expenditures for repayment of debts that represent reasonable and necessary expenses for the production of income   _____

    i. Medical expenditures necessary to preserve life   _____

    j. Reasonable expenditures for the benefit of the child and the other parent exclusive of gifts (for noncustodial parent only)   _____

Total Required Deductions from Income $_____

Net Monthly Income $_____

B. Cash or Cash Equivalents

   1. Savings and interest-bearing accounts $_____

   2. Checking   _____

3. Stocks and bonds   _____
4. Other (specify) _____   _____

Total Cash or Cash Equivalent on Hand $_____

C. Statement of Monthly Living Expenses

1. Household

   a. Mortgage or rent (specify) $_____
   b. Taxes: assessments and insurance   _____
   c. Maintenance and repairs   _____
   d. Heat/fuel   _____
   e. Electricity   _____
   f. Telephone   _____
   g. Water and sewer   _____
   h. Refuse removal   _____
   i. Laundry/dry cleaning   _____
   j. Maid/cleaning service   _____
   k. Furniture and appliance replacement   _____
   l. Food (groceries/milk, etc.)   _____
   m. Tobacco products   _____
   n. Liquor, beer, wine, etc.   _____
   o. Other (specify) _____   _____

   Subtotal Household Expenses $_____

2. Transportation

   a. Gasoline $_____
   b. Repairs   _____
   c. Insurance/license   _____
   d. Payments/replacement   _____
   e. Alternative transportation   _____
   f. Other (specify) _____   _____

   Subtotal Transportation Expenses $_____

3. Personal

    a. Clothing $_____$

    b. Grooming $_____$

    c. Medical

        (1) Doctor $_____$

        (2) Dentist $_____$

        (3) Medication $_____$

    d. Insurance

        (1) Life $_____$

        (2) Hospitalization $_____$

    e. Other (specify) _____ $_____$

Subtotal Personal Expenses $_____$

4. Miscellaneous

    a. Clubs/social obligations/entertainment $_____$

    b. Newspapers, magazines, and books $_____$

    c. Gifts/donations $_____$

    d. Vacations $_____$

    e. Other (specify) _____ $_____$

Subtotal Miscellaneous Expenses $_____$

5. Dependent children:
   names and date of birth

_____

_____

_____

_____

_____

    a. Clothing $_____$

    b. Grooming $_____$

    c. Education

        (1) Tuition $_____$

        (2) Books/fees $_____$

(3) Lunches _____
(4) Transportation _____
(5) Activities _____
d. Medical
(1) Doctor _____
(2) Dentist _____
(3) Medication _____
e. Allowance _____
f. Childcare _____
g. Sitters _____
h. Lessons _____
i. Clubs/summer camps _____
j. Entertainment _____
k. Other (specify) _____ _____

Subtotal Children's Expenses $_____

Total Living Expenses $_____

Debts requiring regular payments:

Creditor	Balance	Minimum Monthly Payment
_____	_____	_____
_____	_____	_____
_____	_____	_____
_____	_____	_____
_____	_____	_____
_____	_____	_____
_____	_____	_____
_____	_____	_____

Subtotal Monthly Debt Service $_____

Net Monthly Income $_____

Total Monthly Living Expenses $_____
Difference Between Net Income
    and Expenses $_____
Less Monthly Debt Service $_____
Income Available per Month $_____

Appendix C

Battered Women's Shelters

Alabama

Montgomery Area Family Violence Program
Kiwanis Domestic Abuse Shelter
P.O. Box 4752
Montgomery, AL 36101
205-263-0218

Alaska

Women in Crisis-Counseling & Assistance
702 10th Avenue
Fairbanks, AK 99701
907-452-2293

Arizona

My Sister's Place
961 West Ray Road, #4
Chandler, AZ 85224
602-821-1024

Arkansas

River Valley Shelter for Women
P.O. Box 2066
Russellville, AR 72801
501-968-3110

California

Battered Service Action Center
108 North Bonnie Beach
Los Angeles, CA 90063
213-268-7564

Colorado

VOA–Brandon Center
1865 Larimer Street
Denver, CO 80204
303-620-9190

Connecticut

Stamford Domestic Violence Service, Inc.
65 High Ridge Road
Suite 378
Stamford, CT 06905
203-357-8162

Delaware

Child, Inc./Family Violence Programs
11th & Washington Street
Wilmington, DE 19801
302-762-6110

District of Columbia

House of Ruth—"Herspace"
651 10th Street NE
Washington, DC 20002
202-347-2777

Florida

Sunrise of Pasco County, Inc.
P.O. Box 928
Dade City, FL 34297-0928
904-567-1111

Georgia

Safe Homes of Augusta, Inc.
P.O. Box 3187
Augusta, GA 30914-3187
404-736-2499

Hawaii

YWCA Family Violence Shelter
3094 Elua Street
Lihue, HI 96746
808-245-6362

Idaho

Women Against Domestic Violence
P.O. Box 323
545 Shoup Avenue
Idaho Falls, ID 83401/2
208-525-1820

Illinois

Harriet Tubman Shelter
4844 South State Street
Chicago, IL 60609
312-924-3152

Indiana

The Caring Place, Inc.
Brick Yard Plaza
426½ Center Street
Hobart, IN 46342
219-464-2128

Iowa

YWCA Battered Women Program
35 North Booth
Dubuque, IA 52001
319-588-4016

Kansas

The Crisis Center, Inc.
P.O. Box 1526
Manhattan, KS 66502
913-539-2785

Kentucky

The Center for Women & Families
P.O. Box 12526
226 West Breckinridge
Lexington, KY 40583
606-255-9808

Louisiana

Capital Area Family Violence
Intervention Center, Inc.
P.O. Box 2133
Baton Rouge, LA 70821
504-389-3001

Maine

Caring Unlimited York Co.
Domestic Violence Center
P.O. Box 590
Sanford, ME 04073
207-324-1802

Maryland

Heartly House, Inc.
P.O. Box 831
Frederick, MD 21701
301-662-8800

Massachusetts

Transition House (Harvard)
P.O. Box 530
Cambridge, MA 02138
617-661-7203

Michigan

YWCA Domestic Crisis Center
25 Sheldon SE
Grand Rapids, MI 49503
616-451-2744

Minnesota

Harriet Tubman Women's Shelter
P.O. Box 7026
Powderhorn Station
Minneapolis, MN 55407
612-827-2841

Mississippi

Domestic Violence Project, Inc.
P.O. Box 286
Oxford, MS 38655
601-234-7521

Missouri

SafeHaven
P.O. Box 11055
Kansas City, MO 64119
816-452-8535

Montana

Butte Christian Community Center/Safe Space
1131 West Copper
Butte MT 59701
406-782-8511

Nebraska

Friendship Home
P.O. Box 95125
Lincoln, NE 68509
402-475-7279

Nevada

Temporary Assistance for Domestic Crisis Shelter
P.O. Box 43264
Las Vegas, NV 89116
702-646-4981

New Hampshire

Rape & Domestic Violence Crisis Center
P.O. Box 1344
Concord, NH 03301
603-225-9000

New Jersey

The Safe House
P.O. Box 1887
Bloomfield, NJ 07003
201-759-2154

New Mexico

The Albuquerque Shelter for Victims
   of Domestic Violence
Box 1336
Albuquerque, NM 87103
505-247-4219

New York

Sanctuary for Families
P.O. Box 413
Times Square Station
New York, NY 10108
212-582-2091

North Carolina

Family Services of McDowell County, Inc.
P.O. Box 1572
Marion, NC 28752
704-652-6150

North Dakota

Family Crisis Shelter
P.O. Box 1893
Williston, ND 58801
701-572-9111

Ohio

Templum House
P.O. Box 5466
Cleveland, OH 44116
216-631-2275

Oklahoma

Domestic Violence Intervention Services
1419 East 15th Street
Tulsa, OK 74120
918-585-3143

Oregon

Bradley-Angle House, Inc.
P.O. Box 14694
Portland, OR 97214
503-281-2442

Pennsylvania

Women's Shelter of Greater Pittsburgh
P.O. Box 9024
Pittsburgh, PA 15224
412-687-8005

Rhode Island

Women's Center of Rhode Island, Inc.
45 East Transit Street
Providence, RI 02906
401-861-2760

South Carolina

Sistercare, Inc.
P.O. Box 1029
Columbia, SC 29202
803-765-9428

South Dakota

Children's Inn
409 North Western Avenue
Sioux Falls, SD 57104
605-338-4880

Tennessee

Serenity Shelter
P.O. Box 3352
Knoxville, TN 37927
615-971-4673

Texas

Genesis Women's Shelter
Drawer G
Dallas, TX 75208
214-942-2998

Utah

YWCA of Salt Lake City
322 East 300 South
Salt Lake City, UT 84111
801-355-2804

Vermont

Women Helping Battered Women
P.O. Box 1535
Burlington, VT 05401
802-658-1996

Virginia

YWCA—Women's Advocacy Program
6 North 5th Street
Richmond, VA 23219
804-643-0888

Washington

YWCA Emergency Shelter for Women
and Children in Crisis
1118 5th Avenue
Seattle, WA 98101
206-461-4882

West Virginia

Family Crisis Center
P.O. Box 207
Keyser, WV 26726
304-788-6061

Wisconsin

Women's Resource Center
P.O. Box 1764
Racine, WI 53401
414-633-3233

Wyoming

Teton County Task Force on Family
    Violence/Sexual Assault
Box 1328
Jackson, WY 83001
307-733-7466

Appendix D

Typical Real Estate Provision

The Husband and Wife are owners of a certain parcel of real estate improved with a single-family residence, commonly known as 123 Main Street, Anytown, which has been the marital residence of the parties. Both parties have and each party does by these presents warrant and represent that the marital residence is free and clear of any monetary liens and encumbrances except for a first mortgage in the sum of approximately $100,000 with First Home Mortgage Corporation and unbilled general real estate taxes. The parties represent that said mortgage and real estate taxes not yet due are the only liens which currently exist on the premises. If it is hereafter determined that any other lien or encumbrance has been placed against the marital residence by the actions or inactions of one of the parties, then he or she will take all appropriate steps to remove such lien or encumbrance including, but not limited to, the payment of any creditor.

The Husband shall be entitled to claim as a deduction from

income for the 1993 year, mortgage interest and taxes relating to the period beginning January 1, 1993, through December 31, 1993, inasmuch as the Husband has made all such payments during such period of time. From that date forward, the Wife shall be entitled to claim as a deduction from income all items relating to the marital residence, including mortgage interest, and taxes, beginning January 1, 1994, and forward.

The parties hereby acknowledge that the Husband has vacated the marital residence. Upon entry of a Judgment for Dissolution of Marriage, the premises shall be placed in tenancy in common, reflecting the Husband's 40% interest in the premises and the Wife's 60% interest in the premises. Until the marital residence is sold and the closing has taken place, the Wife shall have exclusive use and occupancy of said residence. The Wife shall be solely responsible for payments to become due after January 1, 1994, including but not limited to mortgage, real estate taxes, insurance, and utilities.

The parties shall consult regarding the necessity of any repairs and/or replacements as to the home in order to preserve the market value of the property. The cost of any such repair and/or replacement shall be remitted 60% by the Wife and 40% by the Husband. If either party fails to remit payment of said expense at the time of incurring said expense, that party's share shall be reduced from his/her share of proceeds at time of sale and shall be tendered to the other party.

The parties have agreed that the marital residence shall be placed for sale on or before June 1, 1996, unless otherwise mutually agreed in writing by the parties. The Wife may place the property for sale prior to June 1, 1996, should she so desire. Upon consummation of the sale of the premises, whether prior to or subsequent to June 1, 1996, the proceeds thereof shall be disbursed in the following order and manner:

A. The payment of real estate brokerage commissions, if any; attorney's fees for closing; seller's title expenses, costs of title insurance; costs of county and state revenue stamps; costs of discharging the first mortgage; real estate taxes and all other costs, expenses, and prorations of a nature and in an amount customarily and ordinarily incurred in connection with the sale of residential real estate property shall be paid from gross proceeds;

B. To the Wife, sixty percent (60%) of all sums remaining after payment of the foregoing amounts outlined in "A";

C. To the Husband, forty percent (40%) of all sums remaining after payment of the foregoing amounts outlined in "A."

Each party agrees he or she will not cause, suffer, or permit any lien or encumbrances to be placed on or against the marital residence so long as they remain co-owners other than those referenced herein. In the event either party, by their actions or inactions, permits or causes a lien or encumbrance to be placed on or against the marital residence, any such amounts shall be reduced from the share of proceeds that party would have otherwise received at time of sale.

The Wife shall report as income an amount equal to 60% of the gross proceeds of sale, less 60% of the adjusted basis of said property and 60% of other deductions therefrom as shall be permitted by law, subject to such deferrals and/or exclusions as may be allowed by law. The Husband shall report as income an amount equal to 40% of the gross proceeds of sale, less 40% of the adjusted basis of said property and 40% of other deductions therefrom as shall be permitted by law, subject to such deferrals and/or exclusions as may be allowed by law. To the extent of each party's respective liability under this paragraph, each shall indemnify the other and hold the other harmless with respect to any and all taxes, penalties, interest, and/or other expenses which may be assessed against one party by virtue of the other party's failure to declare his or her respective share of the foregoing sales proceeds.

Upon the happening of a specified event leading to the sale of the marital residence (June 1, 1996, or such earlier time as the Wife desires to sell said property, or at such other time as the parties may mutually agree), the parties shall each have the option to purchase the interest of the other in the marital residence. In the event that both parties desire to purchase the interest of the other, and cannot reach an agreement regarding same, then the premises shall be placed for sale on the open market and the premises shall be sold to a third party.

The sale price shall be determined by agreement of the parties. In the event the parties cannot agree upon a sale price, then each party shall select and pay for an appraiser to affix the fair market value. The final valuation shall be the median sale price determined by comparison of both appraisals and shall be binding upon both parties. The final value shall be diminished by 7.5% to allow for commissions and ordinary seller's charges which would be incurred in the sale of the home to a third party.

The resulting figure (net market value) shall be reduced by the balance then due on the mortgage now existing on the property, resulting in a figure to be known as net equity. Net equity shall be divided 60% to the Wife and 40% to the Husband, and the party desiring to purchase the residence shall be entitled to purchase the share of the other for an amount equal to the share of the other of net equity.

The party desiring to purchase shall have 45 days from the date of the appraisal or an agreed-upon price to obtain financing; thereafter, unless extended by agreement, the home shall be listed for sale, and net proceeds of sale shall be disbursed to the parties as provided in this document.

Appendix E

Typical Visitation Provision

The Mother and Father agree to reasonable parenting time for the Father. (Parenting time may be referred to as "visitation.") These periods of time shall be scheduled as follows:

a. Every other Friday at 5 P.M. to Sunday at 8 P.M.

b. During such weekday periods as are mutually agreeable to the parties.

c. Major holidays will be as follows: The Mother shall have the children on Mother's Day, Christmas Eve, and the Mother's Birthday. The Father shall have the children on Father's Day, Christmas Day, and the Father's Birthday. In even-numbered years, the Father shall have the children on Easter, New Year's Eve, and New Year's Day. In odd-numbered years, the Mother shall have the children on Easter, New Year's Eve, and New Year's Day. In odd-numbered years, the Father shall have the children on Thanksgiving Eve and Thanksgiving Day. In even-numbered years the Mother shall have the children on Thanksgiving Eve and Thanksgiving Day. The children's birthdays will be spent with whichever parent has visitation with the child that particular day. The Mother shall have the children on Memorial Day and Labor Day in even-numbered years; the Father shall have the children on Memorial Day and Labor Day in odd-numbered years. The Mother shall have the children on July 4 in odd-numbered years; the Father shall have the children on July 4 in even-numbered years.

d. The father shall have two weeks of visitation during the summer. The Father shall notify the Mother thirty days in advance of this two-week visitation period. The Father shall supply the Mother with a telephone number, address, and vacation itinerary prior to summer visitation. Additionally, during this summer visitation period the children will be permitted daily telephone contact with the Mother.

e. Any visitation which the Father misses for good cause, such as illness or work schedules, shall be rescheduled and made up within thirty days of the date on which visitation was missed.

f. Transportation costs relating to visitation shall be borne by the Father, so long as the Mother resides in the state. In the event the Mother no longer resides in the state the parties shall attempt to reach a mutual agreement regarding the costs of transportation relating to visitation. If the parties cannot reach such an agreement, either party may bring an appropriate action such that a court of competent jurisdiction may make such a determination.

Index